1000 Years of Sobriety

1000

Years of Sobriety

20 People × 50 Years

William G. Borchert and Michael Fitzpatrick

HAZELDEN®

Hazelden
Center City, Minnesota 55012
hazelden.org

LIBRARY OF CONGRESS CATALOGING-IN-PUBLICATION DATA
Borchert, William G.
    1000 years of sobriety : 20 people x 50 years / William G. Borchert and
Michael Fitzpatrick.
        p. cm.
    ISBN 978-1-59285-858-3 (softcover)
    1. Alcoholics Anonymous. 2. Alcoholics—Rehabilitation—United States
3. Alcoholics—United States—Biography. I. Fitzpatrick, Michael, 1959-
II. Title. III. Title: One thousand years of sobriety.
    HV5279.B67 2010
    363.29′2092273—dc22

                                                            2010017832

Editor's note
These stories are edited transcriptions of interviews. Alcoholics Anonymous,
AA, the Big Book, the *Grapevine, AA Grapevine,* and *GV* are registered trade-
marks of Alcoholics Anonymous World Services, Inc. Hazelden offers a variety
of information on chemical dependency and related areas. The views and inter-
pretations expressed herein are those of the people interviewed and are neither
endorsed nor approved by AA or any Twelve Step organization.

18   3 4 5 6

Cover design by David Spohn
Interior design and typesetting by Cathy Spengler

Contents

Authors' Note

THERE IS AN INSIGHTFUL SANSKRIT PROVERB that proclaims: "Yesterday is but a dream and tomorrow only a vision, but today well lived makes every yesterday a dream of happiness and every tomorrow a vision of hope."

What a gift it must be to experience this way of life for more than fifty years, as have those whose stories are contained in this book.

Looking ahead, five decades can seem like an eternity— 600 months; 2,600 weeks; 18,250 days; 438,000 hours; or 1,576,800,000 seconds. But looking back, five decades can seem like a series of fleeting moments we may either cherish or disdain.

However, lived well in sobriety, fifty years can produce an abundance of good works, a plenitude of loving friends, the sharing of great spiritual wealth, and the creation of a solid path for others to follow as they tread that road of happy destiny.

It has been an enormous privilege to write this book and the stories of twenty people from around the world who have lived the Twelve Steps of Alcoholics Anonymous one day at a time for more than fifty years—and are still carrying this great message of recovery to others.

Spending time getting to know these wonderful members of the fellowship has not only been a truly rewarding experience, but an honor as well. Each one of them clearly demonstrates the adage: "Freely you have received, freely give." Saved from an almost certain alcoholic death more than fifty years ago, they have spent these past five decades or more carrying the message to others—a mission that has undoubtedly touched thousands upon thousands of other alcoholics and their families.

Although their stories were at times sad and tragic, they

turned out to be some of the most inspiring testimonies one could possibly imagine. Now, with the publication of this book, their experiences will continue to bring hope and unconditional love to the world long after their service on this earth is finished. For that we can all be grateful.

It is our wish that you will be inspired by their stories and challenged by their accomplishments.

BILL BORCHERT AND MIKE FITZPATRICK

Foreword by Sandy B.

THIS REMARKABLE COLLECTION of the personal stories of twenty present-day AA "old-timers" could not be more timely or valuable. As the fellowship of Alcoholics Anonymous reaches its seventy-fifth year, authors Bill Borchert and Mike Fitzpatrick make available to the two million members of AA a treasury of insight into AA's past fifty years that could not be achieved in any other fashion. Further, since the early sobriety of all these members coincided with the later days of the earliest AA old-timers and founders, including Bill Wilson, this book creates a bridge for us to experience the entire AA story.

I take personal delight in commenting on this rare collection because many of these men and women have become personal friends. Some were heroes of mine in my early sobriety. They are living icons in the particular areas of the country where they presently reside. Sadly, the stories of many other icons have faded with their passing. I know of several whose stories I deeply wish had been reduced to writing. There is something comforting and enduring about the written word. Tapes and CDs of AA talks are stimulating and valuable. But the written story brings a sense of history and permanence with it.

While reading, we can take our time to reflect on and enjoy particular passages. I am sure that, as time passes, we will always be glad that we added this book to our personal collection. It will be available to stimulate and nourish our memories any time we pick it up and settle into our favorite chair with it for an hour or so.

To our newer members, I urge you to assemble your own collection of AA-related books and definitely to include this volume. Until you know and experience the entire AA story, your sense of belonging will be limited and tentative. Gradually, though, you will come to realize that you and your story are part of AA history. What is history but a collection of stories? As the total AA story comes alive in and through you, you will begin to see yourself as a small but vital part of one of God's greatest miracles and can delight in the realization that this story is a part of you as well.

I would like to thank the authors for enriching my life with this marvelous collection and for their tireless efforts on behalf of the fellowship.

SANDY B.
Tampa, Florida

Foreword by Howard P.

IN THE BOOK *ALCOHOLICS ANONYMOUS*, author Bill Wilson promised, "We shall be with you in the Fellowship of the Spirit and you will surely meet some of us as you trudge the Road of Happy Destiny."

Many of us have already had the privilege of meeting some of the men and women who tell their stories in this wonderful book—who tell what it was like, what happened, and what it is like now after more than fifty years of continued sobriety.

These men and women who have experienced "pitiful and incomprehensible demoralization" and now walk in "the sunlight of the spirit" are still active in the fellowship of AA. They continue to be among us, to speak with us on a one-to-one basis in meetings, on the telephone, and at AA conferences and roundups.

The lives of the twenty alcoholics presented in this book provide solid evidence that the practice of AA's spiritual principles have worked for them for fifty years or more. And they will tell you, in their own way and in their own words, "If it can work for me, it can work for every one of you."

I am grateful for the role I have played in helping to bring this book to fruition. I want to join in thanking these twenty sober members of Alcoholics Anonymous with more than a thousand years of sobriety for sharing their lives with us.

HOWARD P.
Gilbert, Arizona

1000 Years of Sobriety

> *"I wanted to kill myself, but I wasn't about to walk ten more miles to do it."*

THE STORY OF CLANCY I.

A pleasant voice comes over the intercom and says, "Please keep your seatbelts fastened until the airplane comes to a full and complete stop at the gate and the captain has turned off the fasten seatbelt sign." I fumble around to make sure I have everything ready to depart the plane. A three-hour flight east is not nearly as comfortable as it used to be.

Once I deplane I'll meet my host, who will take me to a hotel that will be my home for the weekend. This weekend's agenda looks very familiar. It begins this evening: dinner at five with several members of the conference committee, AA meeting at eight, and a dance to follow.

In the morning I will be presenting a workshop on sponsorship, followed by lunch. At two they have me scheduled for an AA history talk, then a four o'clock old-timers panel. In the evening there will be a banquet where I am the guest speaker.

On Sunday morning I'll be up at five to catch a direct flight back to LA. Later in the day I will be giving one of my sponsees his twenty-year sobriety birthday cake. This may seem like a busy weekend; however, it has become routine for me.

I spend my weekdays at the "Midnight Mission" on LA's Skid Row, where I've been working since 1974. In the evenings I attend AA meetings around the LA area and attempt to spend time with my family. Today I am very fortunate to be able to enjoy being a husband, father, grandfather, and great-grandfather.

Over the past fifty-one years I have been grateful to have a very active sober life. My membership in Alcoholics Anonymous has given me opportunities beyond anything I could have ever conceived—to befriend and sponsor some of the wealthiest and most famous men and women in the world, including movie stars, business owners, sports celebrities, and rock stars.

But please don't mistake my association with celebrities as bragging. I'm also friends with and sponsor many people who have drunk up almost everything in their lives and in many cases are homeless. Unfortunately, I have seen people from both groups die tragic alcoholic deaths. Alcoholism does not discriminate, and it shows no favorites.

As you can probably already tell, Alcoholics Anonymous has transformed my life from what it was more than sixty years ago when I first came through the doors of the fellowship at the age of twenty-two.

I was an only child born and raised in the small city of Eau Claire, Wisconsin. I was introduced to God at a very early age in the Norwegian Lutheran Church, which was about as tough as it gets when it comes to religion. I knew with certainty that God was a powerful, punishing figure that dwelled off in the clouds somewhere. He was just waiting for the opportunity to catch me sinning so he could strike me dead. It got to the point that whenever the word "God" was mentioned, I would cower. I learned both fear and guilt at a very early age.

When I was fifteen years old, I told my mother I was going to take a bus to Superior, Wisconsin, to visit my aunt. The truth was that I was going to hitchhike to San Francisco to join the military. As luck would have it, I was picked up by a guy who drove me almost the entire way to California.

My driver, a navy man returning to his ship, told me I wouldn't be able to find any way into the military because I was not yet sixteen. He suggested I go to the Coast Guard office on Market Street and apply for seaman's papers. I went there and lied about being sixteen, but they still needed a parent's signature. I went around the corner, and "my mother" signed the form.

I was issued temporary seaman's papers and referred to the National Maritime Union. World War II was raging, and they were looking for merchant seamen. That very night I was aboard a ship carrying loaded torpedo warheads to the South Pacific. I remember lying in my bunk that night, homesick and knowing I had made a mistake. One of the seamen came in with a bottle of whiskey and passed it around. He looked down at me and said in a gruff voice, "You want a snort, Junior?"

By that time a million thoughts were racing through my head. I had made a promise to my mother and grandmother that I would never drink alcohol. I was a movie buff, and in the movies the good guys never drank; only the bad guys. Of course, the religious people had also convinced me that drinking was a curse. With all those thoughts going through my mind, I knew I didn't want to drink. However, I looked up at him, reached for the bottle, and said in my squeaky, adolescent voice, "You're damn right I do."

I'll never forget that first drink of whiskey. It burned my mouth, my throat, and my stomach as it went down, and on the way back up it burned my stomach, my throat, my mouth, and his shirt. I felt terrible, not because I had gotten sick, but because the other men were laughing at me. It was the most humiliating and embarrassing moment of my life. It was truly dreadful!

From that day on, I knew where to find a bottle, and I would drink when nobody was around just to see if I could keep it down. I wanted to prove to my shipmates that I was a man. The day finally came when it stayed down.

I relate to the way that many others in AA describe their first drink experience. I, too, felt a warm glow from the inside out. It was a feeling of omnipotence, unlike anything I had ever experienced. In retrospect I would have to say that I took my last drink for exactly the same reason I took my first drink. I drank to feel on the inside how other people looked on the outside.

When I was seventeen, I went into the United States Navy. At the end of the war, as the time neared for my discharge, I took the GED examination. It allowed me to earn my high school diploma so I could enter college at the University of Wisconsin. I married while in college, and we had a couple of children.

By 1949, I was drinking too much to stay out of trouble and was even put in jail briefly on several occasions. I heard about Alcoholics Anonymous and decided to check it out. There were eight men at the meeting I attended, all well over forty. I was still in my early twenties, so I decided I was too young to be an alcoholic and left AA.

My first job after college was as a sportswriter. It didn't pay very well, and with a growing family I continued to look for something better. In time, I got a job writing sales correspondence, which led me to that company's advertising department. I eventually got hired at an advertising agency and traveled around the country writing for them. I became quite the successful young advertising executive. Throughout all that success, my drinking continued to increase, as did my feelings of superiority over everyone else. I can see now that alcohol had become my best friend.

For the next nine years I bounced in and out of AA, with brief periods of sobriety. But even so, I managed to be jailed twenty-nine more times during those years and lost everything a man could lose. Once while I was in jail my infant son died, leaving me with feelings of immense guilt.

In 1956, I successfully committed suicide in El Paso, Texas, where we were living at the time. I say "successfully" because I had literally died. I sat in the car with the motor running and the garage door closed. By the time my neighbor found me and pulled me out of the garage, my heart had stopped beating. Thank God he was able to resuscitate me.

I was taken to the city "psycho ward," where I spent the next three weeks. During my mental evaluation the doctors learned that I had had some drinking problems. They talked with both me and my wife about my drinking, then determined that I could not simply be released. Consequently, on October 14, 1956, I was committed to Big Springs State Hospital. The diagnosis was not alcoholism. It was schizoid personality disorder with no prognosis of recovery. It really meant a life sentence with no way out.

After I had been there just two weeks I escaped, not realizing it was an escape-proof facility. However, Texas is very flat. I think I could be seen running in my white bathrobe from about fifty miles away, in any direction. Needless to say, I was caught. For the next three months I received electric shock therapy. It wasn't given to me as a "punishment." I'm sure they thought I must be really disturbed or I wouldn't have tried to escape. I can assure you, this treatment slowed me down. I never tried to escape again.

After the course of shock treatments, I didn't even remember coming to Texas. The last thing I could remember was playing piano for drinks in a San Francisco bar. With determination I decided I was going to get out of that hospital legitimately, and I did. I became a model patient. Even in the "nuthouse" I had a strong streak of perfectionism in me. I was going to be the best patient they ever had. I became the founder of the *Big Springs Hospital Newspaper* (it had a short life) and was its first editor and publisher. I also directed the Christmas pageant; it was a beautiful thing, if you overlooked the craziness.

While I was in the hospital, I met a guy named Les Ross. He spent a great deal of time talking with me about my problems. He told me that he thought I was an alcoholic. With respect, I explained that I couldn't be. Even though I drank excessively, something more was wrong with me. By then I had convinced myself I was different.

The hospital had just opened an alcoholic ward. Les arranged for me to attend the AA meetings there. I believe it was an experiment to see if a mental patient could respond to AA therapy. Things went along just fine, so I was permitted to go with a group to outside meetings in Midland and Odessa. I was even able to give five-minute talks at those meetings.

After about six months in the hospital, I was released and returned to El Paso, where I still had two AA sponsors. The night before I was to celebrate my first birthday in sobriety, I found myself in Juarez holding a drink and waiting for the clock to hit midnight before I downed it. I knew I wasn't an alcoholic. There was something very sick inside of me, but it wasn't identifiable and it certainly was not alcoholism.

So I decided to control my drinking. It actually worked for a short period of time. I found a job with an advertising firm in Dallas. My pregnant wife, three daughters, and I moved to Dallas, where she gave birth to our fourth girl. It was the summer of 1958. My drinking soon got worse.

I lost my job, got another one, and lost it, too. I came home very drunk on a Friday afternoon to find the house empty. My wife had begun attending a new fellowship called Al-Anon. She didn't just leave and take the kids; she took everything. The house was vacant, with not even a rug left. She left no contact information, and I had no way to get in touch with her.

For the next couple of weeks, I stayed drunk while doing some work for a guy in Wichita Falls. When this writing job was finished, he gave me a hundred dollars and sent me on my way. Another friend gave me his car, wanting me to deliver it in Los Angeles. On the first day I made it as far as El Paso, got drunk, and looked up an old sponsor so I could curse him out.

I managed to get thrown in jail for drunkenness in Juarez later that evening. Once out, I headed for Phoenix. In Phoenix I somehow lost the car with all of my belongings, including my ID. I was locked up in the city "drunk tank" and was so drunk I vomited onto a guy's bunk before falling asleep on the floor. When the guy realized what I had done, he started kicking me in the face, leaving me bloodied and without my front teeth. Because of my experience with psychiatrists, I immediately knew what was wrong with this man. *He was overreacting.*

The next morning I was released after paying a small fine. There I was in downtown Phoenix, broke and broken and not knowing what to do. I fished a dime out of my pocket and placed a series of collect phone calls to everyone I could think of. Nobody accepted my calls, and once again, I pondered suicide.

I was told there was an AA club up the road, so I walked about fourteen blocks until I found it. I sat in the Arid Club, coming off the alcohol and shaking. I was so sick. I spent a long day at that clubhouse without a drink. I finally prevailed on convincing one of the members to "lend" me twenty dollars for a rehab bed.

As soon as I had the money, I ran to the bus depot, hoping to get to Seattle, but I only made it as far as Los Angeles. I was in such bad shape that I was even evicted from the Midnight Mission, a Skid Row facility. There was a little scuffle and I was literally thrown out. As I was flying through the air, I wanted to tell them, *"Don't you know who I am? My picture has been on the front page of the* New York Times *for my achievements. I've been on the faculty of a major university, and my ads can currently be found in most major national magazines.*" (It's hard to say all this while in midair.)

I remember lying on the ground looking up at the two guys who had tossed me out. I shook my fist and said, "I'll be back; you haven't seen the last of me."

Only God knew then that this hopeless, helpless, insane, drunken loser of a man would make his way back there fifteen years later as the managing director, sober and restored as a human being through his grace and the Twelve Steps of Alcoholics Anonymous.

The morning I was thrown out of the mission, I tried to sell a pint of blood. I was rejected because the iron level in my blood was too low. I needed to do something. It was raining outside, and I was finished. At that point I wished I *was* an alcoholic, but I knew that when I stopped drinking things always got worse. Drinking couldn't be the problem. My emotions were so intense when I wasn't drinking that it just had to be a mental problem.

After walking seventy-one blocks to the AA club in a cold October rain, I tried to look sincere. It didn't take long for the guy at the door to size me up. He said, "All right, you can come in. Now go in the back room and sit there and wait for the meeting. Don't let anyone know I let you in, because I think you're a phony."

I thought, "Okay, I'm in. Now I'll get one of these pukes to be my sponsor and in a few days I'll con him out of enough money to get me back on my way to Seattle." It was Halloween 1958; I had no idea it would be my sobriety date.

The challenge in front of me was not quitting drinking. If drinking was my only problem, all I would need to do was quit and my problem would be solved. I discovered it was much more intricate than that. Alcohol anesthetized the pain that was so prevalent when I was sober. In my mind it had become the solution.

I believe one of the greatest drawbacks for a "slipper" like me is the knowledge attained while bouncing in and out of the program. I knew the AA Big Book. I had read it twice. I could recite the Steps from memory. I even knew most of the phrases and slogans. I had ridiculed all that spiritual bunk and other nonsense from AA people.

There I was, starting all over, knowing I would have to listen to the same things once again. But this time I would have to try to believe them. The only reason I went back was because there was no place else to go. I had tried everything over the past nine years: religion, psychoanalysis, and institutions. AA was undoubtedly the last house on the street for me.

It was terribly difficult in the beginning, because I was so sick. All I could do was go to meetings. I went several times a day and was given the opportunity to live in an abandoned car outside the 6300 Club. I knew I had to try to make it in the program, for I feared it would be my last chance at life.

As I progressed and things began to get better, I still struggled with my relationship with God. I couldn't let go of my attitude and fears regarding religion that I had held since childhood. It was hard for me to see myself returning to that God, and it was the only image of God I knew.

Then one of the guys in AA said, "Kid, you don't need to return to God. You just need to find somebody you can trust." For a while that was my sponsor, Bob; then it was the group. Slowly, by doing the things I was taught, I awakened to the philosophy of Alcoholics Anonymous. I came to believe in it by following through with everything, even when I didn't understand it or agree with it, even when I thought it was stupid.

I finally developed my own concept of God from the things I respected. The one tangible I could define was intelligence. The auto mechanic who lifted the hood of my car understood how it worked and fixed the problem. I respected him for his intelligence. After months of searching and probing, I was able to come up with a concept of God that was personal to me, a Higher Power I could pray to.

I remember one day thinking about a television antenna that picked up a signal and created a picture. The picture was carried to everyone equally. Similarly, God sends goodness, serenity, peace, and love to every person. If the television was working properly and fine-tuned, the picture was brilliant. This helped me to see that during times when I was not feeling love, serenity, and peace, it was because I was out of adjustment. The transmitter sending the signal was fine; I just needed to turn the knobs to better tune it in. I had to take part and make those adjustments.

By following the directions of my sponsor and becoming teachable, I would be able to see the picture clearer. I began to get rid of my resentments and fixed the things I needed to fix. I started to mend lost and broken relationships.

Taking this course of action gave me a role and a responsibility in my recovery. My actions led to a better life. Those were "adjustment knobs" for me. This concept became the foundation for my sobriety. Through this impression of God, I was finally able to understand the Twelve Steps of AA.

During my early days of sobriety, progress was slow, sometimes painfully slow. It didn't come easily for me. When I was six months sober, a friend helped me to get a job doing dishes at a deli on Sunset Boulevard. On my fourth day of work, my boss came to me and said, "We have to let you go. Here's your check."

I protested and asked, "How can you do this to me? I've lost everything, and I'm trying to get back on my feet. I have been to an AA meeting every night. I'm being honest with everyone and trying to do all the right things. I'm searching to find my kids so I can send them something. I have been doing my best to follow a spiritual program. How can you do this to me?"

He looked up at me and said, "Well, I don't know about all that stuff. You just don't wash enough dishes."

I left the deli planning once again to commit suicide. I decided that this time I would walk to the ocean and drown myself. I walked and walked many miles to where I figured the ocean should be, then finally stopped at a gas station and asked for directions. The guy said, "It's about ten more miles down Wilshire, kid." That created a dilemma for me. I wanted to kill myself, but I wasn't about to walk ten more miles to do it.

I found a pay phone and called Bob B., who was attempting to be my sponsor. He was a great guy and liked to get straight to the point. Perhaps he developed this skill in his career as a motion picture actor and radio personality.

Of course, I began by telling him how unfair things were, and went on and on with my complaints. I whined about how hard it was and how I missed my family. I told him, "I hate living in a car. I don't get enough to eat. And AA just isn't working for me."

He replied rather sternly, saying, "Listen, you punk! Why don't you write your Fourth Step?"

My response was not very enthusiastic. I mumbled, "In my judgment, I'd be better off dead."

"If I wanted your damned judgment, I'd come down and stick my head in the car window. Your judgment has you sleeping in a car. Now you need to follow some directions and *get busy!*"

By that time I was so mad I walked back up Wilshire Avenue, found some paper and a pencil, then began writing a Fourth Step inventory. Afterward, nothing seemed to change. I still had to go back and sleep in the abandoned car. I was still hungry, jobless, and missed my kids. There was only one thing I proved by doing the inventory and that was that it didn't work—I wanted immediate results. It's interesting that I might have done this Step for the wrong reason at the time (my anger toward Bob). However, as it turned out, the anger was enough of a motivator for me to become willing to take action.

About a month or so later, I again felt like killing myself. That time it was because I realized that if what I was hearing at AA meetings was true, then what I had believed all along was a lie. I couldn't face it. In desperation I did my Fifth Step with Bob. It took a long car ride along the ocean, but I got it all out.

Slowly and sometimes painfully, I began to do the work that taught me how to live a sober life. It was not done by doing the things I agreed with. It was done by doing things that were apparently illogical, nonapplicable, and having nothing to do with my specific problems. The actions I took through the Steps of Alcoholics Anonymous became the tools that led me to freedom and sobriety.

When I was five years sober, I was grateful to get my family back, and we made a home together. We even added a son to our family. Many good things began to happen once I learned this new way of life. The good things have caused me to need AA more than the challenges have. It's a funny thing, but rewards and accolades have added new complications to my life or, if you will, to my sobriety. Positive experiences have always caused me more problems than negative ones. Yet I learned that it is through our difficulties that we have spiritual growth.

Today I feel truly alive. I'm so grateful that I have been restored to a respectable human being. I never knew how to be that because I was so busy comparing how I felt to how you looked. Whenever I do that, I'm the loser. I would really like to tell you how proud I am of my children and grandchildren, but that would take hours! So many wonderful events and people have touched my life during the past fifty-one years. If I had hundreds of pages, I would list them all by name!

Through my journey in life I have seen much advancement in our culture. It's amazing how creative we are as a society. With all of these changes one would think that the AA program would have to change to keep up with the times. Yet AA works today exactly as it did when it first started almost seventy-five years ago. It is still hope and encouragement from one alcoholic to another.

Medicine, science, and religion have worked to find the answer to the question: "Why do some people become alcoholics?" In the meantime, AA has defined alcoholism in an acceptable way and offered a solution to the problem. Through the Twelve Steps of Alcoholics Anonymous, alcoholics in varying degrees of illness have been able to arrest their illness and live happy, productive lives.

Perhaps it works because the Twelve Steps provide a program of action. The alcoholic moves from a condition of self-absorption—where he can only see himself as a "victim"—to a life of service. The spiritual principles of AA lead the alcoholic to be of service to others. The Twelfth Step states: "Having had a spiritual awakening as the result of these steps, we tried to carry this message to alcoholics, and to practice these principles in all our affairs" (*Alcoholics Anonymous,* page 60).

That is exactly why you will find me traveling to another city next week to carry the message. Between now and then you will find me at my home group or down at the mission. I know as I was taught: I must continue to give away what has been freely given to me. Before I wrap this up, I would like to share a story.

Every five years, Alcoholics Anonymous holds an international convention. I've attended all of them except the first two. The very first one was held in Cleveland in 1950. At that convention the Traditions were accepted by the fellowship as a part of AA. Historically speaking, that act has proved to be one of the greatest things to happen to AA.

On that same day another significant event took place. Co-founder Dr. Bob gave what is referred to today as his "farewell message." He was very sick at the time and knew he would live only a short time longer. The cancer had taken over.

Dr. Bob stood up to the microphone and suggested that we "keep this simple." He then made several very important points: "Let's not louse it all up with Freudian complexes and things that are interesting to the scientific mind, but have very little to do with our actual AA work. Our Twelve Steps, when simmered down to the last, resolve themselves into the words 'love' and 'service.'" He continued, "Let us also remember to guard that erring member—the tongue—and if we must use it, let's use it with kindness and consideration and tolerance."

He made a few more brief comments, suggesting that we remember to pat the new man on the back and take him to a meeting or two. He also warned us against complacency. I have enjoyed listening to recordings of Dr. Bob's words over the years.

In 1970, I was invited to speak at the international convention in Miami. Bill Wilson was scheduled to speak on Friday night, but an announcement was made that he wouldn't be able to make it. He was too ill. Everyone, including me, was very disappointed.

On the way back to my hotel that night, I said to a guy, "Gee, it's really too bad we won't be hearing Bill."

This man replied, "Clancy, let me tell you something. Before this conference is over, we will hear from Bill W." This guy was an old-timer from Ohio. I just smiled, knowing he must have missed the announcement.

Saturday came and went and, of course, Bill W. never showed up. He was in the hospital, very close to death. On Sunday morning we were sitting in the auditorium while Dr. Jack Norris was speaking. Someone walked up to the podium and said something to him. He stopped speaking and music started playing. He said, "Folks, we have a special guest who just arrived."

Bill Wilson was pushed out from behind the curtain in his wheelchair. At the podium, he slowly pulled himself erect. It took almost everything he had, his body was so frail, but he stood there looking out at the sea of faces and gave a short talk. He then returned to the hospital by way of ambulance.

Once I had witnessed this, I understood why the old-timer was so sure Bill W. would speak at the convention. It was Bill's last time to let the membership know how much he loved them.

What remarkable men Bill and Dr. Bob were! Because of their efforts and this God-inspired program of AA, millions of people have found sobriety and a new way of life. The examples set by both of these founders right up to their final days have been an inspiration to me for many years. As I continue to travel around the world sharing my experience, strength, and hope with others, as best I can as a fallible human, I pray my example will help reflect the love and dedication of those who traveled the road before me.

AA is really just one alcoholic talking to another alcoholic. My mission has been, and continues to be, to carry the message to others even when they don't yet quite believe it, knowing that when someone takes the action necessary, the day will come when they too can be *safe, sane, and sober.* It is in giving that we receive, and I have received abundantly for fifty-one years.

"Booze didn't bring me happiness,
but it did kill the pain."

THE STORY OF BILL D.

When it comes to the Traditions of Alcoholics Anonymous, count me in as a traditionalist who believes in telling what it used to be like, what happened, and what it's like now. I'm not much of a pontificator, although I do enjoy talking about all the wonderful blessings of sobriety, which have been rather plentiful in my life. Well, actually, that's true in the lives of most AAs who live this program to the best of their ability.

Anyway, as an old traditionalist, I believe we need to share our "drunkalogs" so that newcomers especially can identify and realize that they're not alone, can come to understand that there is a way out no matter how far down they've gone, and finally can witness in the person sharing his or her story the tremendous miracle of Alcoholics Anonymous. Each day that I live, I become more and more certain that AA is truly one of God's greatest miracles.

I was born on October 16, 1931, and raised in East Harlem, which was back then one of the roughest and poorest sections of New York City. It was mainly populated by black people along with a constant influx of Irish, Italian, and Puerto Rican immigrants. It was also the Mafia headquarters at that time, so at a very early age I found myself running errands along Pleasant Avenue for the likes of Three Fingers Brown, Tommy Lucchese, and the Genovese mob.

My parents were newly arrived Irish Catholic immigrants. My mom worked as a maid in hotels while my father was a part-time longshoreman, a pool hustler, and a full-time raging alcoholic. He was always broke, mean, and very abusive to my mother. By the time I was eleven, my older brother, younger sister, and I had lived in nine different run-down tenements. We would come home from school and discover we had just been dispossessed one more time. What was left of our furniture would be out in the street along with the cockroaches. It was kind of rough. We were also in and out of foster care, which was then called the Society for the Prevention of Cruelty to Children. I came to hate my father and had a hard time forgiving him when I finally got sober.

When I was around six years old, my mother started sending me to the neighborhood saloon to bring my father home. That's where and how I had my first drink—at the age of six at my father's favorite watering hole. Everyone in the joint would be loaded and would want to have fun with the little kid. One day they filled up a fishbowl with beer, handed it to me, and told me to chug the whole thing. While it may be difficult to believe, I managed to get most of it down before my father carried me home—a staggering drunk with his little drunken son in his arms. So that's how it started and that's how it continued for the next eighteen years.

It was the Depression era, and everybody was hungry and in need of practically everything. I had to fight for whatever I got—and I mean literally fight.

The neighborhood would put on these boxing matches called Harlem Smokers. I'd get into the ring with other kids seven, eight, nine years old, and we'd whale the daylights out of each other as the crowd cheered us on. I was an angry, tough little kid and did pretty well despite the black eyes and bloody noses. The harder we fought, the more coins people would toss into the ring. That was our prize money. I'd pick up as many coins as I could and go out and buy food for the family.

Some of us joined what was called the Ash Can Crowd, people who would toss ash cans through store windows at night and run off with whatever they could grab. My brother and I would also rip BX cable out of abandoned tenements along with zinc, copper wire, and toilet bowls. We survived by selling the stuff through the mob scrap dealers. I'm certainly not proud of doing these things, but that's how we lived during those tough times in Harlem. My mother would be at work all day slaving for pennies, my father would be at the bar drinking them away, my little sister would be back in foster care, and my brother and I would be on the streets, drinking and hustling.

Not long ago, while reminiscing with one of my sons, he asked, "Dad, I was wondering if there was anything in your life back then that made you happy." I thought long and hard about his question. I reflected back on some of the crazy things I did as a teenager that I thought were fun and exciting at the time, but then realized they were always done at somebody else's expense. That's why they didn't make me happy. I told my son that was probably one of the reasons why I also drank so much, because I continued to hurt so many people. Even the drinking didn't make me happy, but it did kill the pain.

Although my drinking was progressive, my survival instincts kept me going. Strangely enough, they also helped me develop my innate entrepreneurial instincts, which paid big dividends for me when I finally sobered up. But at this time in my life, I thought I had to do it all myself through my own self-will. Back then, I had little or no contact with God and didn't even consider what he would want me to do or how to live.

In addition to my illegal hustling activities, I also had legal businesses like selling newspapers and flowers on street corners and shining shoes along Third Avenue. Those jobs taught me how to stake out a territory and fight for it regardless of the strength of your competition. I fought many a tough brawl with guys who wanted my busy street corner, because I was cocky and pugnacious by nature—sure signs of a future alcoholic.

Also, around the age of nine or ten, I was hired by two gorgeous hookers to tend bar in their small hard cider joint. They put a platform behind the bar so I could reach customers and gave me a stained apron to wear to make me look older. I'd serve all the horny Irish drunks and hustle them at the same time. There was a cot in the back room with a drop cloth covering the doorway. Even at nine, I knew what went on back there for two dollars a pop.

Usually after a busy night, the hookers would need something to help them get back on their feet the next morning. I'd stop by on my way to school and siphon some of the hard cider out of the big barrels into a gallon jug to make it easier for them to handle. Then I'd drink a bunch of it myself and show up in class with a glow on.

How I managed to finish grade school I'll never know. Perhaps, even through my often blurry eyes, I could see what life was like for so many other fellows in my neighborhood, and I didn't want to wind up the same way. A lot of the older guys I was running numbers with for the Mafia, for example, were being arrested and shipped off to places like Dannemora Prison and Sing Sing penitentiary. But then during my last year in grade school, something happened that turned out to be rather fortunate for me in the long run.

One summer afternoon, I was racing toward the East

River with a bunch of rowdy pals to have a swim when I was struck by a bus. I wound up in Mount Sinai Hospital with a broken leg. When I was there, a priest from the neighborhood dropped by to talk with me. He said I was wasting all my God-given potential and suggested I do something about it before it was too late. He suggested going to a particular high school in West Harlem that had a great reputation for straightening out young guys like me. He so impressed me for some reason—maybe it was his obvious love and caring—that I decided to follow his advice.

Going to that school turned out to be the best thing I ever did, and it even slowed down my drinking for a while. Although the priests and brothers who taught there smacked me around a lot and I almost got thrown out two or three times, I made it through four years, got a great education, and graduated, which made me feel good about myself for the first time in a long time.

After graduation in June of 1950, I decided to take that famous geographical cure, so I hitchhiked to Florida. It was a very bad decision. One night I was having a drink at a bar in a black neighborhood when I was arrested for violation of the segregation laws. I was arrested by "M. M.," the sheriff in Deerfield Beach, and was told the penalty for my action was thirty days in a chain gang as well as a five-hundred-dollar fine. This time the sheriff gave me a break and simply threw me out of town with a warning never to come back. Not knowing where else to go, I returned to New York where, over the next few years, I was arrested eight or nine more times for being drunk and disorderly.

My return to New York also marked the beginning of my first real job. I was hired at the Borden Company in New York City, the outfit made famous by "Elsie the Cow." I was taking home almost forty dollars a week, which was pretty decent money back then, enough to get me started drinking more and more often. I was now almost eighteen. One day I found myself talking with one of the company's prominent lawyers about this fantasy I had of becoming a criminal attorney. Before I knew it, he had me attending St. John's University in Brooklyn, New York, at night on a program supported by Borden.

Despite this great career opportunity, I was drinking more and more and having more consequences. I was going out with this very pretty girl at the time, and she walked out on me. To get more money to drink, I began hocking everything in sight at the local pawn shop—my watch, the family toaster, my brother's suits. Then I started stealing things again, like clocks and furniture from the lobbies of apartment buildings. I can still remember a loveseat I took from one building. It was about five o'clock in the morning, and I was real drunk. I managed to get it out into the street and rolled it all the way down from Ninety-fifth Street to Hungarian Steve's used furniture store. He was closed, of course, but when he arrived at nine o'clock that morning, he found me sleeping it off in this loveseat. All I wanted was five or ten bucks to keep my spree going, but he said, "Get this piece of junk out of here; it's worthless." He then slammed the door in my face.

I was now missing days from work and my university classes and was creating all kinds of excuses for not showing up. One day when I walked into the office at Borden's, my boss's secretary stopped me and asked, "How did your EKG come out?" When I frowned, obviously not knowing what she was talking about, the woman responded, "Your heart attack. You called in yesterday and said you had a heart attack."

It was October 1950; I was a fairly strong, strapping nineteen-year-old kid when I had actually phoned in with the excuse of having a coronary—and not remembering a thing about it. That was the real start of my blackout drinking. Eventually, Borden fired me for chronic absenteeism, which was the result of my chronic alcoholism. I lost a whole string of jobs for the very same reason—because I cared more for the bottle than for anything else or anyone else.

One day that winter, an attorney at the Borden Company, who seemed well aware of all the problems I was having, looked me straight in the eye and asked, "Do you think you might have a problem with your drinking?" Without a moment's thought I answered, "You know, I guess I might have or something." He asked if I would like to come over for dinner and talk about it. I did, and met his lovely wife. They said they would like me to meet some of their friends.

The kind of life I was leading had been catching up with me. I had been slashed by a knife in a street fight, stuck twice in my side with an ice pick, shot at many times by neighborhood gangs, and had almost drunk myself to death more times than I could count. And yet now this lawyer and his wife were seeing something in me that I could not see in myself—that I was powerless over alcohol and needed help.

That night Mansfield and his wife, Ceil, took me to my very first meeting of Alcoholics Anonymous at the Lenox Hill Group in Manhattan. It was February of 1951, and I was nineteen years old. I don't remember much of what was said that night, but I do remember this feeling I had inside, this feeling of being very grateful that I was there. I knew for some strange reason that God had something to do with it, for I suddenly realized how lucky I was to be alive.

There were more than a hundred people at the meeting that night, mostly men, and I knew right from the start that if I stayed there with them, my life would change for the better. As I began to make more meetings, I got a sense that there was something very powerful about this fellowship. One night at the Lenox Hill Group I was introduced to a very short, very pleasant white-haired man with a pair of pince-nez glasses on his nose. He was Dr. William Silkworth from Towns Hospital, where I was told one of the cofounders of AA, Bill Wilson, had a spiritual experience and never drank again. I was also told the good doctor helped the struggling fellowship in many ways at the very beginning.

Dr. Silkworth was a very kind man. I remember him saying to me that night, "I am very happy to see you here. Keep coming to these meetings. One day there'll be a lot of young people like you in Alcoholics Anonymous and alcoholics won't have to hit such low bottoms anymore." Looking back now, his words were almost like a prediction of how, by AAs spreading the message, people wouldn't have to suffer as much or as long anymore from this terrible disease of alcoholism.

He was very encouraging to everyone he spoke to. While not an alcoholic himself, Dr. Silkworth would come to the group and usually be surrounded by a bunch of wives who would keep asking him things like, "What happens if my husband drinks again?" or "What am I going to tell the neighbors now that my husband's stopped drinking?" He would smile and shake his head and tell them to keep coming and just listen.

In addition to meeting Silkworth, I had the honor of meeting Bill myself. I came to learn and love the great history of how our program was founded and grew into the worldwide organization it is today. Bill was a regular at the Lenox Hill Thursday open meeting, and he was Mansfield's first sponsor.

At almost every meeting I would hear that if I was a real alcoholic and continued to drink, I would keep losing jobs, become unemployable, wind up in more jails and nuthouses, get sicker and sicker physically, and then die of this disease if I was lucky. I knew in my heart that they were right, that I had already crossed that invisible line. But the compulsion to drink just wouldn't leave me. So for the next several years I ping-ponged in and out of the program.

The first time I got drunk, I came back to keep a good job someone in the fellowship had gotten for me. I was embarrassed that I had let him down. But this wasn't enough motivation to keep me dry, and I drank again. A year later I came back to meetings because of my mother. She was crying all the time and afraid the cops would come, knock down her door, and drag me off to prison because of all the bad things I was doing once more. The drinking was now out of control, and I was becoming violent, getting into more street brawls, and even being barred from some of the worst saloons in Harlem. I was now twenty-three, and a lot of times I was more dead than alive.

In 1953, things began going downhill rather fast. While I had many blackouts, I can still remember the day I sold blood out of my left arm at the Bellevue Blood Bank for five dollars and went right to a local bar and drank it up. Then I staggered uptown to a small hospital where I sold more blood out of my right arm to buy more booze.

In November 1954, I began bleeding and having convulsions, so my doctor suggested I check into the Rockefeller Institute for Medical Research as a "specimen." That's how they accepted patients back then to do research on, and I guess they thought they could learn something about the disease of alcoholism by putting me through a barrage of tests. I didn't mind, because it was winter and very cold on the New York streets as well as in the doorways where I was now waking up quite often. Between the good food and the medications at the hospital, I began doing pretty well over the next three or four weeks, so the doctors decided to let me go to my mother's for Christmas.

At the hospital, a doctor/psychiatrist had put me on a new drug called Antabuse, which was designed to prevent alcoholics from drinking. It made you extremely ill and could possibly be fatal if you drank with it in your system. Each dosage lasted about three days. I remember my mother giving me some money as a Christmas present to buy some new clothes. She felt since I was on Antabuse I wouldn't use it to drink. After all these years she still didn't know how foxy alcoholics think they are or how stupid they can actually be.

I was about to face the beginning of the end. Some old friends invited me to a Christmas party in Greenwich Village. I went to show them how great I was feeling being sober and healthy again. But seeing all the booze there and the fun going on, I finally had to leave. On the way back to the Bronx, the maniac in my alcoholic brain started working on me. It convinced me that three days had already passed—well, not quite but almost—and that the effects of the Antabuse had probably already worn off. It was close to four in the morning so I told myself, "You can have a few beers and everything will be okay."

I spotted a bar on the corner. I told the cabbie to pull over and invited him in with me for some holiday cheer. He agreed. I put ten bucks on the bar, had a few quick ones, and went to the men's room. When I came back out, most of my money was gone, and the booze I mixed with the Antabuse was already setting me off. I accused the bartender and the cabbie of robbing me. I punched the cabbie and demanded he give me my money back. He ran out and jumped into his taxi. I followed him, leaped into the back seat, and continued to pummel him as he drove crazily down the street.

He saw a police car just ahead and pulled up next to it screaming for help. I jumped out and started to run. The cops shouted for me to halt, then fired about six shots over my head. I got the point and dropped to my knees. I was arrested and charged with assault and robbery in the first degree. When we finally get sober and look back at our lives, we can see those times when God steps in and tries to help us out. This was one of those times.

I had a rap sheet with about ten different charges on it, ranging from drunk and disorderly to assaulting police officers. I was about to face a grand jury when this prosecutor calls me into his office, sits me down, and stares at my rap sheet. He sees that every charge against me was the result of my alcoholic drinking. He hands me the court Bible, turns to me, and says, "Son, we decided to give you a break. I want you to hold this Bible in your hand and swear to God that you'll never drink again in the City of New York. If you do drink again, we'll hit you with an indeterminate sentence in Rockland State Hospital for the slightest misdemeanor."

Now I had never held a Bible in my hands before. The closest I had come to such a holy thing like this was a Catholic catechism in grade school. It made me very nervous because I knew I'd be swearing to God himself. But it was such a good deal I couldn't turn it down. So I swore on that Bible and they let me go. Four days later I got drunk and threw a guy through the plate glass window of a bar. Then I took off for Chicago.

Knowing I had to do something about my drinking or go to jail, a nuthouse, or die, I decided to try AA one more time. I went back to meetings and promised myself I'd make a whole new start in the Windy City. I even got a job with the AC Nielsen Company and began rooming with five others guys who worked there. One night one of the guys pulled a bottle of Jim Beam out of the refrigerator. That's when I learned what it really means to be totally defenseless against the next drink.

While I only showed up at the job three days, AC Nielsen paid me for nine and then fired me. I drifted down to Skid Row in Chicago, living on the streets with bottle gangs and in flophouses with bug-infested winos for fifty cents a night.

One night I came out of a drunken stupor in another flophouse. Aching all over, I had never felt so completely hopeless. I had a cut over my eye, blood on my shirt, and black pus draining from one of my ears, which had been kicked and severely injured in another street brawl. I sat on the edge of my filthy cot and made a decision. I'd climb up to the roof of the building and jump off. That would solve everything. But first I'd take a little stroll and finish the rest of the rubbing alcohol I had mixed with my bottle of orange soda.

It was almost midnight when I crossed the street and headed for the Pixley and Ehlers Café, one of those dump restaurants on Skid Row. My ear was running pretty badly now, so I figured I'd get some napkins and stuff them in to dry it up. You know how drunks like to self-medicate. That's when I saw this tall, stocky man standing under a lamppost. He was wearing a dark coat and dark suit, and when I got a little closer, I saw in the dim light that he was wearing a white collar. He was a Catholic priest.

For some reason I stopped and stared at him. He smiled back. Then he noticed my ear bleeding and said, "You ought to get that ear tended to. It looks bad." I just nodded. "There's a hospital not far from here," he said, so I went to the hospital and had my ear treated in the emergency room.

When I went back to the flophouse in the early morning hours, instead of climbing up to the roof and jumping off as I had planned, I went back to my cot and fell asleep. When I awoke later that morning, my compulsion to drink was gone. I felt a strange kind of peace inside of me. I thought about that priest I had met, his warmth and his caring. While he had said nothing special to me, I knew something extraordinary had happened because of him, for I have never drunk another drop of alcohol since that day—August 18, 1955.

A miracle had happened, no question. God was doing something for me that I could not do for myself. I also knew that I had to get back to Alcoholics Anonymous if I were to stay sober, which I did that very night. I also got a job a few days later working for Manpower at a buck an hour. While it was a menial job, I still needed some better clothes for work.

This little guy named Schwartzie who hired the day laborers told me to go over to Catholic Charities and they would help me out. So I went, and who do I bump into there but the same priest I met just a few nights before on that street corner. His name was Father Ignatius McDermott, better known as Father Mac to everyone on Skid Row, where he dedicated his life to helping alcoholics for more than fifty-seven years before he passed away. He was a saintly man, and I'm pleased to say that we became good friends.

When I tried to thank him one day for the miracle that occurred in my life, he smiled humbly and said we are all simply tools to be used by Almighty God. I was to discover that he was right and that the real reason God had brought me into AA, along with millions of other alcoholics, was simply to help others. I also learned that's what keeps me sober—carrying the message of recovery to those still suffering from this terrible disease and trying to help anyone else in need.

So I got very active in AA, making meetings, making coffee, getting a sponsor, and doing what I was told to do. Also, through my relationship with Father Mac and his great example, I returned to the Catholic faith and have remained an active, practicing Roman Catholic to this very day. It has helped me enormously in my spiritual life, which I first found in the program through the Third and Eleventh Steps. I know, despite more than fifty-four years away from a drink, that my sobriety depends upon my spiritual condition one day at a time, as the Big Book tells me.

After being sober about four years, I met the loveliest woman in the world and married her in 1959. Her name's Ellie; she was a Mennonite girl from a farm in Illinois. Today we have five wonderful children, two sons and three daughters, all college graduates and very special people. For example, one of our sons became a renowned retina specialist and then went off to India and Africa to work with lepers. One of our daughters was the youngest woman invited to join the Young Presidents Organization (YPO). Still another daughter is a successful real estate agent who has been sober in AA for more than eleven years. Our younger son is a computer analyst who does international trade and finance. Our middle daughter is a schoolteacher. God has truly blessed our family and showered us with all kinds of gifts in sobriety.

Shortly after Ellie and I married, we moved to Wisconsin, where I started my first business, an outdoor advertising company. I had worked for one in Chicago, so I had some experience in the field. I became more successful than I ever dreamed. As I said earlier, those entrepreneurial instincts I developed as a hustling youth began paying dividends in sobriety.

I went on to start, build, and sell many other companies over the years, always knowing that these great blessings were gifts from my Higher Power, the fruits of which I have always tried to share with others. For example, my dear friend Father Mac always dreamed of having a large facility near Chicago's Skid Row where he could take better care of the alcoholics and homeless men and women to whom he dedicated his life. Because of my God-given success, I was able to join with others in Chicago to help build such a structure for him— a seven-story building with five hundred beds named the McDermott Center. We opened it after his fiftieth anniversary as a priest, and more than three thousand people came to celebrate the occasion.

I've also been afforded many other wonderful gifts and opportunities in sobriety, like meeting Mother Teresa, helping to start minority-owned businesses, being given three presidential appointments, and writing a best-selling book. I share these good things along with the bad so that my fellow AA members can see that dreams do come true in our fellowship if we work for them and if they are the will of God.

Now at the age of seventy-nine, I also carry the message of recovery through the design and building of affordable residential treatment facilities for alcohol- and drug-dependent individuals and their families. These are facilities with a program based on the Twelve Steps of Alcoholics Anonymous. Because of my own checkered past as a youth, we focus on severely addicted young people and have been filled with joy to watch them recover and rebuild their lives in AA.

I sometimes ask, Why me? I often feel I'm not a very deserving person. I once thought that God didn't really like me for committing all those sins as a supposedly Catholic young man. But in AA I learned that God loves us all regardless of our past and that he is very forgiving. Through the Twelve Steps I found a God that surpasses all understanding.

About twenty years after I got sober, I was driving one afternoon through the beautiful countryside of Tennessee, just north of Knoxville. Suddenly I had this overwhelming feeling of gratitude sweep over me and once again, like back in that Skid Row flophouse in August of 1955, I felt the presence of God—my Higher Power revealing himself to me in a very special way. I had to pull over and stop the car, for the experience was so powerful.

When it was over, I realized one more time that when we alcoholics have a spiritual awakening as a result of the Twelve Steps, our lives will never be the same—and for that I will be forever grateful. Because of Alcoholics Anonymous and a forgiving God, I am now happy, joyous, and free.

"Sobriety as a Christmas Gift"

THE STORY OF ANITA R.

My husband, Jim, and I were both released from the alcoholic ward of New York's Knickerbocker Hospital on Christmas Day in 1952. From that day until Jim's death in 1994, we enjoyed a wonderful life together in sobriety. He had two days more of sobriety than I did. If ever I had an AA sponsor, it was him.

I was one of seven children, raised on a Nebraska farm during the Prohibition era, so there really wasn't much drinking around me as I was growing up. The workers in the fields drank some of the home brew that I helped my mother make, but that was about it. The bootleggers' stuff was quite expensive.

My early schooling took place in a country schoolhouse. Since I was a good student, I was able to graduate from high school when I was just fifteen and got a scholarship to a business school. Before I finished the business school program, a small-town doctor from nearby Kenesaw came to our farm and asked if I would work at his office. Although I had never considered such work before, I agreed to take the job.

My brothers poked fun at me over that whole idea because I was one of those people who couldn't visit someone in the hospital without feeling sick. I soon got over that, thanks to this doctor. On my first day of work, he was preparing to do a tonsillectomy. I got up to leave the room, but he said, "Oh, no you don't. You sit right down there and put your head down." I did as he said and from that day on I never had a problem with a queasy stomach.

After eight years of work in the doctor's office, I decided to enter nurses' training school in Denver, Colorado. The program was at St. Luke's Hospital and lasted three years. World War II was going on when I completed my training. Several other nurses and I decided to join the Navy Nurse Corps.

Up to this point in my life, I rarely drank. Occasionally I would have a few drinks on a date, but that was all. When I entered the navy, however, life quickly changed. Almost immediately someone invited me to the Officers' Club for a few drinks. I accepted and enjoyed it very much. My alcoholism gradually progressed from that point forward. I began drinking at the club regularly, which concerned some of my superiors. One day I was doing rounds with a doctor and complained that I had a sore neck but didn't know why. He quickly said, "Well, I do, and it's a wonder that you didn't break it when you fell off that bar stool last night."

I believe my supervisors thought that if I was given more responsibility, I would be too busy to drink very much. They sent me to Baylor University in Dallas, Texas, where I enrolled in a course to became a nurse anesthetist. The plan to curtail my drinking worked—while at Baylor I was so busy with the program that it left no time for drinking.

Upon completing my training at Baylor, I was stationed

at Corona, California, where the navy had taken over the Lake Norconian Club. The surgeon in charge asked if I had been taught how to do spinals at Baylor. I told him I hadn't, though I had observed them. He said, "Your life here is going to be dull unless you learn how to do them." He taught me the procedure, and I did many after that with no mishaps.

My drinking at this time was pretty well limited to the Officers' Club, and I never drank before going on duty. Only once did I have liquor back at my room. It was Christmastime and one of the nurses had a Christmas tree in her room decorated with little bottles of liquor. One day when she wasn't home I went in, cut off some of the bottles, and drank them. I don't recall if I ever told her what I had done, although I'm sure she knew who it was.

After my time in Corona, I was stationed in Hawaii, where I was the only one in charge of anesthesia. One day, one of my commanding officers saw me walking down the hallway and invited me into his office. He asked me to sit down and told me that he was not reprimanding me, but he was concerned about my drinking. He knew that other doctors saw me drinking in the Officers' Club at night and were aware that I'd be taking care of the anesthesia for their patients in the morning. I'm not sure how I responded, but I probably just told him that I'd do better. By that time, however, my drinking had become a habit, and I didn't cut down.

The hospital was getting ready to close, and the chief nurse from Washington asked where I would like to go for my next duty. She offered Guam, one of the other islands, or said I could go back to the mainland. I told her I would like to go somewhere that had a doctor in charge of anesthesia. I was sent back to Oakland, California, where I had been stationed once before.

Once in Oakland, I was standing in the hallway one morning and the doctor in charge stopped at the drinking fountain. As he walked away, I heard him say, "I don't know why they

don't fill these things with beer. It would be so much better!"
Needless to say, he was very tolerant of my drinking.

Shortly before I was due to leave the service I met and
married my husband, Jim. We met on my ward. He was a
ship's captain and was about to be discharged from active duty
to the reserves. We had our first date on his birthday, February 19, 1950, and were married less than one month later on
March 15 at Treasure Island. We stayed in Oakland until I was
discharged. We then moved to Jackson Heights, New York,
Jim's hometown.

Neither Jim nor I went to work immediately upon arriving
in New York. Actually, we didn't have any real employment
until after we got sober in AA. We were both drinking heavily,
and I had some mistrust toward him—I was concerned that
he was getting more alcohol than me. Although we certainly
had plenty, I wanted it to be even. We had opportunities to so-
cialize and attend lots of parties. I had heard somewhere that
if you drink vegetable oil before drinking alcohol, you won't
get drunk. I learned the hard way that that doesn't work.

The only area in which we were organized and responsible
at this point in our lives was in making sure that we always
had enough to drink. Jim would go to the Brooklyn navy yard
to pick up liquor, so we always had an ample supply. As time
went on we started to realize that this wasn't the way to live.
Jim heard of a doctor in New Jersey who treated alcoholics.

The doctor understood alcoholism and the progressive-
ness of the disease. I agreed to go see him with my husband.
I will always be grateful to that doctor because he really did
understand this illness. He asked both of us many questions.
Then he explained that he could help with our immediate
problem by giving us some nonaddictive medication to help
us relax, but stressed that Alcoholics Anonymous had the real
answer for the alcoholic. My husband's sister was already a
member of AA and doing well. We thought we had learned
enough from the doctor, and we both agreed we would just

stay away from that first drink. We figured that we didn't need AA.

We managed to get by without drinking for a while, but neither of us was working yet and there just seemed to be something missing from our lives. One day we were invited to attend the army–navy game with some old navy friends. My husband, knowing that there would be lots of drinking going on, suggested that we allow ourselves to have "a few drinks" that day and then after the game we could return to our nondrinking ways. This sounded like a good idea to me. Of course, we didn't stop after the game but picked up right where we left off before going to the doctor.

After a while we knew that we had to do something about our drinking, so my husband called the New York intergroup office and got an AA sponsor. At that time there was an AA ward at the Knickerbocker Hospital. It had been started by Dr. Silkworth, the doctor who had cared for Bill Wilson some eighteen years earlier. An alcoholic had to be sponsored into the hospital by an AA member, so my husband's sponsor arranged for him to be admitted for a week. I planned to stop drinking on my own while he was there and told him I'd be sober when he got home.

A couple of days later I found myself drinking in a bar because I had run out of booze at home. I knew that I needed help, and I couldn't let my husband come home to find me in that condition. I called someone I knew in New Jersey who would be able to sponsor me into Knickerbocker Hospital. Then I headed for New Jersey, driving drunk for what turned out to be the last time. I will always remember that I left Jackson Heights, New York, and headed through the Lincoln Tunnel to New Jersey with a flask on the seat. To this day I don't know if I had my last drink in New York or New Jersey.

I learned a lot about AA while at the hospital. I also had the opportunity to meet a wonderful, kind woman, Nurse Teddy R. She helped many alcoholics through her work. It was a five-day program, but they allowed me to leave a few days early when my husband was scheduled for discharge. On Christmas Day 1952, Jim and I left Knickerbocker Hospital as sober members of Alcoholics Anonymous and began our sober journey together. I will always remember this Christmas gift of sobriety and the AA way of life. I couldn't have asked for a better present.

In some respects, AA was very different in 1952. For example, in Jackson Heights there were only two meetings held weekly. One of the meetings was an open speaker meeting where a lot of spouses of alcoholics attended. The other was a Twelve Step meeting. Sponsorship was not really stressed like it is today. Rather, the group did the sponsoring and taught members about the Steps at the Twelve Step meeting.

During my early sobriety, I sometimes received calls from the intergroup asking me to go see ladies who needed help. Normally when going on Twelve Step calls, two members would go together. On one such occasion, however, I went alone because there was no one available to go with me. When I arrived at the home, I knocked on the door several times but received no answer. I tried the door and found it unlocked. Upon entering, I was overwhelmed by the smell of natural gas. The lady had passed out on the couch and the stove burner was left on with no flame. She had done this by accident and was not attempting suicide. The woman survived, began to attend AA, and did quite well. Another lady I called on more than fifty years ago is still sober today and living in Florida.

Both Jim and I found jobs shortly after getting sober. He became a salesman selling industrial paints with South America as his territory. I got back into nursing by working at a doctor's office. We were both active in AA, and I did some speaking around New York when asked.

One evening I was speaking at an AA meeting in one of the suburban communities. I noticed that a man and a woman were whispering to each other while I was giving my talk, which I thought was a bit rude. After the meeting, they came up to me and introduced themselves as office employees of AAWS (Alcoholics Anonymous World Services). They wanted me to join them for lunch the next day. It turned out that the man was the general service office manager, Hank G. The woman was Hazel, a staff worker. During lunch they told me about an opening at the GSO (General Service Office) that they wanted me to consider taking. I was surprised with the offer, but after some thought and talking with my husband, I decided to accept the job. When I told my boss that I was leaving the doctor's office, he said, "I guess if I were to offer you more money, you wouldn't change your mind." He was right; my mind was made up.

At AAWS, I was one of six staff members. Each of us had specific responsibilities, and my first position was to handle inquiries. Much of the mail I responded to came from members in areas that didn't have any meetings established. I would correspond with these people, called "loners," and provide whatever information was available to help them. I also corresponded with prisoners who were interested in starting AA groups.

After I had worked at the office for a little while, I began to receive invitations to speak at various AA conferences. Sometimes I was asked to provide information about the General Service Office, while other times the groups wanted me to give my AA story. These trips took me all over North America.

One such trip to Florida turned out to be a memorable event for me. Although I would generally fly to the events, at the time there was a promotion to take a train, which sounded appealing and relaxing to me. It turned out that part of the promotion was free champagne. My waiter asked me if I'd like some. I pleasantly declined, but he persisted. Actually, he came by several times and really tried to encourage me to drink. Finally I replied in a loud voice, "No thanks! I'm on an alcohol-free diet!" I was sure that would take care of him, but he came bouncing right back, looked at me, and said, "If I were you, I would change doctors." That was the first time anyone had tried that hard to get me to take a drink.

While working at the GSO, I also had the opportunity to get to know Bill Wilson and see him daily. He was a very pleasant person who really cared about the AA members and AA's future. He personally read all the correspondence that was sent out by staff members. I feel fortunate to have known him. I was able to see him as a fellow alcoholic who had a deep interest and concern for what was happening in the AA world. When we would return from somewhere and give him a positive report, he was always very pleased. As I look around AA today, I think that the thing Bill would be most proud of is how sponsorship has developed. It has become such an important part of AA that allows so many people to get a real chance at sobriety.

Another position I held at the GSO was that of conference chairperson. In this position, I was responsible for staying abreast of all the various AA conferences being held throughout the world. I took one unforgettable trip to the Pacific Northwest and Alaska. I knew Bill W. would be very interested to know how AA was doing in those areas. The office was a very busy place, and it was always very gratifying to watch AA expand into more and more areas.

I remember one man very well and like to recount my experience with him. He was from Norway or one of the other Scandinavian countries. He stood there in the office with a smile on his face and said with great enthusiasm, "You know, as members of AA, if we practice these principles in all our affairs, we can make this world a better place to live." Remembering his words, I know how right he was.

Eventually we moved to Upper Montclair, New Jersey, and I commuted to work at the New York office. In time, the office manager, Hank G., left, and once the new manager came on board, I decided it was time to retire. But about that same time I was asked to consider taking the position of volunteer director at the hospital in Montclair. Actually, one of the nuns talked me into accepting the position, which turned out to be very interesting and enjoyable work.

I stayed on at the hospital job until my husband and I decided to move west to Arizona. A doctor had told us that the air in Scottsdale, Arizona, would be better for my allergies. My husband was able to continue doing his job from there.

Through the year, Jim and I both stayed very involved in AA. I also stayed committed to my church. Unfortunately, Jim eventually developed prostate cancer. I can tell you that the most important prayer to me at that time was the Serenity Prayer: "God, grant me the serenity to accept the things I cannot change, the courage to change the things I can, and the wisdom to know the difference." This prayer really helped me through that difficult time with my husband. I was able to care for him at home throughout his long illness.

During Jim's illness, I stopped going to meetings and continued to stay away even after he had died. During this time, I never had a desire to drink and kept living the program principles, but I didn't have the fellowship. Then one day I received a call from a man who had done some work for me. He said, "I've seen books in your house and I know that you are in AA. I have a sister in terrible condition with cirrhosis of the liver. She won't last long if she doesn't get help. Would you please call on her?" She lived in the same housing complex where I did, and I agreed to go and see her. It was near Christmas, and she agreed that she needed help but asked if I could wait until New Year's. I could sure identify with her and told her that would be fine. So on New Year's Day I took her to her first AA meeting. She is still sober today.

Looking back at this event, I'm so grateful to God for his mysterious ways. If I had not received the call to go help that woman, I might have missed out on many years of happiness and fellowship with all of my AA friends. This way of living is so much better than anything I could have expected, and it has kept me from a life of loneliness.

When I see the newer members coming into the fellowship today, I like to give them a hug and tell them that I will say a prayer for them. I tell them that I hope they will find the friendship, peace, and happiness that I've found in AA by practicing the Twelve Steps. This coming January I will celebrate my ninety-sixth birthday, and I still make five meetings a week. My friends take me most of time, but I am still able to drive at night, so I don't have to rely on them. I just go and go!

"An AA Love Story"

THE STORY OF BILL R.

This story begins at Woodlawn Hospital on the South Side of Chicago. There, on April 27, 1922, a baby girl named Janet entered the world. She was born into a home with a father who was a serious alcoholic. He was mentally and emotionally abusive. Janet grew up scared and very insecure, perhaps needing a father image, but always looking for a way out of that life.

Just a few months later, on July 17, little Billy R. was born in the exact same hospital. I was also born into a home with a troubled father. My mother died at the age of twenty-two, when I was only six. My dad remarried, and I had trouble adjusting and accepting our new life. I knew my father had made a promise to my mother before she died. If he remarried and I couldn't accept it, he would allow me to live with his sister. Therefore, my aunt and uncle raised me. I always felt as if I had been abandoned, even though I hadn't been. In retrospect, I know that my perception of things wasn't accurate, but it nonetheless became my reality.

Janet and I grew up in the Chicago area about ten miles from each other. However, we lived in two very different places. At that time most Chicago neighborhoods were divided by ethnic culture, and each area was very different. I grew up in Hamilton Park, while she was raised in South Shore. We never met until after high school.

During my childhood I appeared to be a fairly normal kid, but I never felt that way. I had intense feelings of inadequacy, inferiority, and loneliness. When I was about seven or eight, reading became my escape. I read everything I could get my hands on, but my favorite was "hero" books. The library allowed me to check out five books at a time, and I did that as often as I could. Reading filled my evenings, since my aunt wouldn't allow me to play outside after dark. She believed that kids got in trouble hanging out at night. I could only stay out past eight if there was a baseball or basketball game.

During high school I was interested in sports though I never played on a school team. I did participate in city and park leagues. Basketball was probably my favorite sport. I also enjoyed softball. It was a little different back then—we played with a sixteen-inch ball.

One year I decided to join the YMCA swim team. Our team won the state championship that year, even though I wasn't very fast. I quit swimming because it was a winter sport. After swimming I had to take a cold shower and then walk home. I was frozen by the time I got home and kept catching colds. Swimming just didn't work out for me.

After high school I got a job at the Northern Trust Company bank. That's where I met Janet when I trained her for her job.

The bank basketball team that I played on was city champion that year, and a dance was planned to celebrate. I didn't have a date yet, so some friends from work suggested I ask Janet. I turned to her and said, "Hey, do you want to go to the dance with me?" She said, "Yes," and we danced together for the next sixty-four years.

Those days were wonderful. We were just two normal nineteen-year-olds dating and having fun. Yet we both still carried emotional baggage from our childhoods. We loved going out for ice cream and hanging out with other couples after work. We were together about a year before we had our first son and got married.

Shortly after the wedding, I joined the army and was sent to France. It was the summer of 1944 during the invasion of France. That's when the drinking began. I've always said the army got me started drinking and the navy got Janet started. Drinking was an everyday thing for me during my three years in the army. It became a habit before it became a problem.

Janet's situation was quite different. She was living in a small apartment with her mother and our son. There was a navy special training center nearby. Janet's cousin was a chief petty officer who had recently returned from the South Pacific. He and some of his friends at the training center took Janet out for drinks—and she started on her own road of alcoholism.

At some point during my three years in the army, my drinking began to get out of control. For a while I thought it was just normal drinking because everybody was doing it. When I was scheduled for discharge from the army, we returned to Hampton Roads, Virginia. Just before we docked, an aircraft carrier making a maiden run from Europe arrived. The passengers from the carrier had been given our quarters, so we had to wait on our ship while they were processed.

When we were finally released, we headed to the train station and the next leg of our destinations. I was set to be discharged from Fort Sheridan Army Base in Illinois. All the guys going there were put on the same train. It worked out to about forty guys per car. I was the train car commander for our group.

We pulled into Cleveland for a three-hour layover and decided to walk to the Howard Johnson's. I was responsible for getting all the guys from my group back to the train on time. But we were having a blast—the civilians were buying us drinks—and we sort of lost track of time.

Finally, I got everyone together and we lined up and marched back to the train station. When we got there, the train was gone. The guy had forgotten to tell us when it was leaving, so it wasn't our fault. We headed right back to the Howard Johnson's bar and got ourselves pretty well snickered up.

After a while I knew we had to get back to the train station, so off we marched again. When we got to the platform, the conductor was talking to two military police he had called. There was a complaint about a couple of sailors, and he wanted them thrown off the train. The MPs explained to him they had investigated the claim and the girls with the sailors said there was no problem. The sailors hadn't done anything wrong, so there was no reason to throw them off the train. The conductor replied that he was sick and tired of all the drunken servicemen and he wasn't going to take any more of their crap.

After eavesdropping on their conversation, I decided that when I boarded the train, I would knock the conductor off the platform. And that is exactly what I did. Then I boarded the train and sat down with my men. All forty of us in the car had weapons. We couldn't put them in our duffel bags because they might be stolen, so we kept them in our jackets. Of course the guns weren't loaded.

I looked out the window and saw all sorts of shore patrol and military police coming for us. So we all sallied forth with our pistols and had a donnybrook.

I woke up in jail. The tank jacket I was wearing had a cut

from just under my neck down to just above my waist. Apparently somebody had gone after me with a knife but fortunately had only cut my jacket.

The lieutenant and the MPs came in and asked me how I felt. I told them I felt fine. They went on to explain that I had gone crazy fighting and had beat up a paratrooper that night. They told me they even had to put the paratrooper in another cell because I wouldn't stop. Just then a voice from the top bunk said, "The hell you did, I've been sitting up here afraid that the son of a bitch was going to wake up."

There I was, a guy who never got in any trouble while overseas. My troubles started when I returned home. I seemed to live in a fantasy world when I got home from France. Maybe I had been doing that all my life. I went back to my old job at the bank and continued to drink. That was when I started to experience blackouts and do some strange things while drinking.

One day a bunch of guys from the outfit stopped in at the bank, and after work we went out drinking. At the bar that night there was a guy running around telling everyone that he was in World War I. He wanted us to know because we all wore a little pin of a "ruptured duck" that signified we were in the service.

The guy bought drinks for us, since we were veterans. He went on and on telling his stories and raising hell with everyone. One of my friends asked me what I would do if the guy gave me all the crap he was giving everybody else. I told him I'd just knock him flat.

Sooner or later Mr. World War I made his way over to us and started telling us a story. My friend, Corporal Buckle, told him the marines weren't in that battle. That immediately started an argument. After a few minutes, I reached for a beer bottle and busted it over the guy's head.

I turned back to continue drinking, only to find the owner standing over me with a gun pointed at my face. One of my pals pulled out a knife and held it up to the owner's throat. He asked me if he should slit it. I told him no, we could handle it like gentlemen. I suggested that the bar owner pick out a champion and the champ and I would go out in the street and settle it once and for all.

The owner got a little Puerto Rican kid from the kitchen, and we walked outside. That kid proceeded to beat the daylights out of me. He was quite a fighter and wore big rings. While he was beating me, the rings were cutting my head and face. The whole time we were surrounded by five of my buddies. The only reason they didn't jump in was because I wouldn't let them.

After a while the kid got weak from hitting me, and his arms wore sore. I asked him if he had had enough. He said yes, so we walked back into the bar with my arm around him. He told the bar owner that we were all friends now, and we got back to drinking. I didn't realize the extent of his punishment on me until the next day when I tried to comb my hair.

Despite my heavy drinking, my home life was good. I joined Janet and her mother in the small apartment they had shared with our son while I was in the service. Over the next few years we had more children and I finished my education. I attended Loyola University for one year and then earned degrees in economics and finance from DePaul University.

While attending Loyola, I continued working at the bank. It made for some very long days. Sometimes I would be quite late coming home because I would stop for a few drinks.

One day I picked up a pie for my wife. It was her favorite, a banana cream with nice thick meringue. I knew she would love it. I stopped at a bar at about 5:30 and took the pie in with me. I didn't want to leave that beautiful pie in the car! Of course everyone in the bar was encouraging me to cut the pie and share it. I resisted their requests and moved on to the next bar. I actually hit several more bars that night, all with the same response to my pie. It was as if I had to spend my night protecting her pie.

I finally made it home at four o'clock in the morning, and my ungrateful wife yelled at me and raised hell. She made me so mad, I took that pie and threw it at the wall. Of course by then the meringue was like glue. The pie stuck to the wall and slowly, one piece at a time fell to the floor. *That* was a fun night we had together.

On another occasion it took me two days to get home. My wife was furious, so I told her that even though I was exhausted, I would be a good husband and take her out. We went to the neighborhood bar. All the regular drunks were home with their wives. I was at the bar with my wife, and she was not happy. She started yelling at me, keeping it up even after we got home. I got pretty sick of it, but not enough to stop drinking.

After graduation, I worked in sales for an insurance company and moved up rapidly. We moved to Park Forest and bought a nice three-bedroom home. I became a department manager and was in charge of training and motivating other salespeople.

The company wanted me to get my "chartered life underwriter," which is the highest designation in the life insurance business. It would have helped the company and done a lot for my career. They gave me time off and sent me to Northwestern University so I could complete the course. But instead of attending classes, I went to bars and drank. My priorities were all messed up; drinking had taken over.

By that time Janet had become a daily drinker herself. She was perhaps a functioning alcoholic, as she and her mother took care of the children the best that they could. We often had parties at our home in the evening. Drinking had really become a significant part of our lives.

My family was always very important to me, and I tried to do the right things with my five children. It went back to those feelings of abandonment that I carried throughout my childhood. I always made sure they went to church, even though I wouldn't go.

I could continue telling of my drinking escapades, but that wouldn't add anything to this story. The truth is that I had never been punished for any of the things I had done. The law would let me go, and I would just continue with the same behaviors. When I lost one job, I would find a new one. When Janet was mad at me, she would get drunk and get over it.

Even without serious consequences, I was feeling worthless. My drinking, or rather my alcoholism, had progressed to the point where I was remorseful for the things I had done and was doing. I was getting into trouble with expense accounts at work and covering up with lies. I felt like I was failing my family and that I had become a loser. It was during those times of deep regret and remorse that I just wanted to die. I wanted out of this life! I had been drinking to forget, but I could no longer forget. The feelings became overwhelming when I wasn't drinking. But even when I was drinking, I couldn't handle the reality that my own failure was more than I could stand.

On January 3, 1957, I woke up on the floor of another woman's house. Her husband was there, too. I knew she had made some phone calls but I didn't know they were to AA. I had never heard of AA but before I left, I asked her to give me the phone number. Right then I called AA and went home.

About two hours later a couple of fellows showed up from AA. I wasn't very impressed with either of those guys. One of them kept shaking his head up and down like he was goofy, and the other one wanted to tell me about hiding bottles in his locker at the steel mill. I thought there was no way I was going to hang around with Goofy and the guy from the steel mill. Of course my ego was telling me that I was better than them. But I *was* at the end of my rope. We had already lost our home because I couldn't afford it, and I was about to lose everything else.

The guys wanted to take me to a meeting, so I agreed to go along. We went to an open speaker meeting in Chicago Heights. The meeting reminded me of church. I wasn't impressed, and

I don't know what the speaker even said. I remember there were a lot of people there, but it wasn't for me. I could hardly wait to get out. Then a guy came up and introduced himself and said that he lived near me and wanted to give me a ride home. He drove a big Packard automobile and knew Mayor Daley. He had played cards with the president of the United States! I had more in common with him and liked him right away. While driving me home that night, he suggested that I go to a closed meeting. I immediately began to explain why that wasn't a good idea. My business had just started up and really needed my attention . . . He gave it to me really good. He poked me with his cigar and told me in perfect Yankee profanity exactly what my problem was. Now, I could have decked him because I was thirty-four and he was fifty-four. But instead I started to laugh.

We went to a closed meeting in Chicago Heights called Homewood Seventeen. Most people today would never make it in Homewood Seventeen. The meeting would start on Friday night about 8:00 or 8:15. Somebody would tell another person he was running the meeting that night. People sat around and talked about how their day went or about resentments and how to get over them. I don't think that group even had a Big Book; they were all about fellowship. Don't take a drink and do go to meetings.

The meeting lasted until around midnight with food after the meeting. Keep in mind, there were quite a few Catholic members who couldn't eat meat on Fridays. After midnight, however, it was Saturday. The ham sandwiches weren't brought out until then so the Protestants didn't eat them all. After the meeting, people would just hang out or play cards. The fellowship was great for me and exactly what I needed.

One Friday I showed up early, and one of my favorite guys that I really respected was already there making coffee. He was a former marine in World War II. After the war he had problems with flashbacks. If he had them while drinking, he turned violent. I had made him one of my heroes. He had been sober a couple years at that time, and I had about ninety days.

I walked up the stairs that night, not looking very happy. He said, "What's the matter, kid?" I told him my story and all that was going on. He looked at me and said, "Well, what are you going to do about it?" I gave him the only honest response I could think of and said I was going to part his hair with a tire iron. He said, "Well that's one way to do it, but don't drink while they take you to jail." So I said to him, "What would you do about it, wise guy?" His answer was, "I'd pray!" Hearing that statement from him was truly amazing for me. I was learning from people who were living the program.

That early period of AA for me was what I call so-dry-ity. It's a lot better than being drunk but it's nothing like sobriety. Not drinking and attending meetings gave me so-dry-ity, but the Steps and my relationship with God has given me sobriety.

One thing I did from the very beginning was to try to help other guys and get involved with Twelve Step calls. When a call came in, they would call me. We ended up with an AA phone in our house. Usually two of us went on the calls. Sometimes during the day it was hard to get another guy, so I would go alone. I was so new when I started doing this that I had to ask my sponsor what to tell them.

He said to tell them how long I'd stayed sober, even if it was only three weeks. And he told me to get the guy to a meeting. He explained that I wasn't the message, only the messenger. If I was able to get him to a meeting, God would talk to him through the group or somebody there. Even today I believe that if I took a guy thirty days sober with me to talk to a drunk about getting sober, the drunk would want to talk to the guy with thirty days' sobriety rather than me with over fifty years. Both Bill Wilson and Dr. Bob got the new men doing Twelve Step calls right away. They knew that by doing so, the new guys would stay sober.

One afternoon I was sitting outside an AA meeting with John H. He and I were friends and had both been sober about one year at the time. John was the nephew of the mayor and had been fired from a great job at the city recording office.

Before AA, John and I drank together. He used to take a briefcase full of various licenses with him into the bar and he and I would sell them. Of course, the mayor found out and that was the end of John's job. I had been fired for commingling funds at my company. John told me that he could never again get a job in politics. I said that I would never find a management job with a legitimate company again. We were both exactly right that day, based on everything we could conceive and had experienced up to that time.

Yet three years later I was the district manager in charge of the Midwest territory for one of the largest publishing companies in the United States. John was an elected representative for the State of Illinois. The message I want to get across here is that if you stop drinking, your life will get better. But if you stop drinking and work the Steps, *you* will get better.

Until I began to take action and try to live by the tenets of the program, I was very limited in my growth. Once I tried to live the program, I started growing. Hopefully even today I remain teachable.

In my early sobriety, one of the guys I was sponsoring also had an alcoholic wife. He asked me what we were going to do about our wives' drinking. I told him I wasn't going to do anything. "If she dies, then she dies. I've got enough trouble with me." He said he wasn't having that attitude, that his wife was going to change.

As it turned out, he went back out drinking and never returned to AA. He and his wife got a divorce, and she spent the next seventeen years living a horrible existence until she finally died drunk while taking a bath. That's why I always tell people when I'm speaking from the podium, "If you're gonna drink, don't bathe. It will kill ya."

Because I didn't try to promote AA to Janet, she found her sobriety one year after I did. She lived the rest of her life as a sober member of Alcoholics Anonymous.

The AA program suggests that we find a God of our own understanding, and I found mine in Jesus. My life has been transformed through AA, and today I get to do God's work in AA.

Shortly before Janet passed away, she was diagnosed with Alzheimer's disease, and I was given the privilege of caring for her. The experience of being needed in that way is something that men don't usually get to have. The wife or mother usually takes care of the kids, the scrapes, and the cleaning up. I was able to benefit in ways I would never have known simply by being of service to this beautiful lady, wife, and mother of my children whom I loved and adored.

Janet was also Christian and was ready to go home to be with God. One day as I was holding her, she became cold, and I knew that she had died. I fell to my knees and reminded God that in the Bible, he had raised the dead, and all I wanted was two more weeks with Janet. The blood began moving through her body again and she got warmer. But I realized then that she was ready to go and I was being selfish. I prayed again, knowing that I had made a mistake and needed to accept his will. I asked God to please take her. She was gone within the hour.

I think it is important for me to say that right until the end, Janet continued to be an active, involved member of Alcoholics Anonymous. In both of our lives AA worked 100 percent. By that I mean neither of us ever found it necessary to drink after we came into AA. Although we both had tremendous gratitude to God for our sobriety, we never forgot that our recovery was contingent upon our willingness to participate in the AA program. The Big Book (page 85) tells us that "what we really have is a daily reprieve contingent on the maintenance of our spiritual condition."

So the love story continues each day. I now know how to love and how to be loved. My life is dedicated to service, and I'm kept busy. My dance card is always full. I've been blessed with excellent health, and I continue to be grateful. I hope that you have enjoyed reading my "AA Love Story" because I've sure enjoyed living it.

"You look real good on the outside,
but how are you really on the inside?"

THE STORY OF CECIL C.

I've been known as "Cec" all my life. Only a few American friends call me Cecil.

As I reflect on my childhood, I remember never liking responsibility. I avoided it whenever possible. For example, at the age of sixteen I joined the Canadian army to avoid the responsibility of high school. On my first evening in the service, some of the older guys took me downtown to a beer parlor where I had my first drink. After more than a few, I recognized I was smarter, wiser, and knew more about living than even my new drinking pals. Thus began my drinking career, and I loved it right from the start.

My army career looked promising. I became an instructor while still sixteen, but this did not mix well with my developing alcoholic ego. At the age of seventeen, between my ego and my drinking, I was thrown out of the army.

Upon returning to my home community of Prince Albert, Saskatchewan, I found a job at an aircraft factory. For a seventeen-year-old, I began making very good money, especially in 1942. I never thought my drinking or my ego was a problem because my life seemed normal to me. While I knew that I was drinking more than other people, I thought it was just that I had a greater capacity for drink than most. Soon my job began to demand too much responsibility from me, and once again my natural response was to run. So at age eighteen I enlisted once again in the army. I had to lie about any previous military experience, a move that I thought was sheer genius. They believed me, and this time I began to show some real promise. I was even being considered for a commission, but once again my drinking, coupled with my fear of responsibility, led to another early discharge. Still, I never even considered that my drinking had become a serious problem.

I returned to my hometown again and got a job in the advertising department of a local newspaper. The job afforded me better-than-average wages, and despite my heavy drinking, others soon recognized that I had potential for the business. The newspaper decided I was ready for more responsibility, which of course signaled me to leave.

This time I joined the navy and tried to keep my drinking under control. I attended officers' training camp and really wanted to become a commissioned officer. After officers' training I went to sea as a gunner on a naval merchant ship, sailing—and drinking—all over the world. By now drinking had become the top priority in my life. It didn't matter where I was or what my responsibility. The only thing that mattered was that I got drunk, and I did. In the navy I met many people in many places around the world. I didn't think there was anything wrong with me, but I could drink more than most other people I met.

We were now in World War II, and I remember sailing

to Australia once with a load of cargo that turned out to be Canadian booze. Once we arrived, we unloaded most of it but stashed a bunch for ourselves. The day we got around to drinking it, we almost created a disaster. Our ship was ordered to haul supplies to the American forces on New Guinea. We expected Japanese aircraft attacks, but they didn't happen on the way there. We were able to deliver the supplies and headed back to Australia.

While on our way back, some of our Canadian aircraft were ordered to escort us in. Of course, by this time the booze had made its way around the ship, and everyone, including the captain and the gunnery officer, were drunk. Still fearing an attack from the Japanese, we were all scared as our own aircraft approached. Suddenly our drunken gunnery officer told us to open fire on them. I was in charge of this big forward gun, and we were all shooting like crazy. All of a sudden our captain realized that we were shooting at our own planes. Luckily, we were too drunk to hit them, but still he got really panicky. He grabbed the big megaphone, looked down at me, and screamed, "Cec, fire!" So I did what I was told. I kept firing, not realizing his order was to "cease-fire."

Even though my drinking continued to progress, I found time to marry a girl from my hometown and managed to stay in the navy long enough to receive an honorable discharge. Returning home, I celebrated the end of the war, the beginning of the Korean War, and right on through the end of that war, too. Of course, by that time I barely needed a reason to drink. I started losing jobs and traveling down the destructive road that many alcoholics have traveled. I hadn't yet reached my twenty-fifth birthday.

Shortly after turning twenty-five, I started a business with a partner. It only lasted four months because of me and alcohol. On the very same day that I lost my business, I lost my wife and my two daughters. I had attended my first Alcoholics

Anonymous meeting by this point, and I've often wondered how different things might have been had I stayed on from the start. Back then, however, I thought AA wasn't for me because I saw too many old guys there. I felt I was too young and had a lot of drinking years left. I thank God today that I only lasted two more years.

During my last year of drinking I became a fighter. I'd fight anyone. In fact I had seventeen fights that year and seventeen knockouts—I lost every one of them. The last time, I ended up in the hospital near death, beaten to a pulp by a 265-pound guy. I probably weighed 135 pounds. While I was in the hospital the doctor told me that there was nothing that he could do for me but patch me up. He said I was an alcoholic, that I needed help, and he called Alcoholics Anonymous himself.

Shortly after that, two men showed up at my hospital room and began telling me the AA story. I knew one of them from my days in the army. He had recently been released from the penitentiary after serving five years for a violent burglary. He had found AA inside the prison. The other guy had been known as the sloppiest drunk in all of Canada. When he walked in, his hair was combed and he wore a nice suit, white shirt, and shined shoes. These two guys didn't have to talk at all. All they had to do was stand there, because I could tell that something had happened to them.

The Saturday morning I was released from the hospital, I went directly to a little café in Prince Albert to meet these AA people. I'll never forget that morning because I'm a guy who loves nice clothes, and you should have seen the way I looked that cold January day, wearing the only clothes I had with me at the hospital. My "fight clothes" included a shirt without buttons and a raggedy topcoat. I sat in the restaurant as other members of AA started to arrive, and they all made me feel welcome by saying things like, "We've been saving you a chair."

Later that day they picked up my wife (who was giving me

another chance) and me and took us to an AA meeting. I hope I'll never forget that night. It was a Saturday night, which was usually a party night for me. I thought the party was over, yet these people were all having a good time. I couldn't believe they were doing it without booze, but I didn't catch any of them drinking!

They had a little gathering and then a meeting. The evening lasted until about one in the morning, at which time one of the guys approached me and said, "Cec, in AA there are no 'musts' but there is a meeting here in this clubroom tomorrow morning and *you must* be there." I was there! I'm glad that they talked with me this way. I was only twenty-seven years old, the youngest member of Alcoholics Anonymous in the province of Saskatchewan, and I needed their direction. Since that night, I have never had to have another drink of alcohol.

After about a year of going to Alcoholics Anonymous meetings, even with all the "pats on the back" and the excitement of being sober, I suddenly felt a void. I was getting tired of hearing "Easy does it," "Don't worry about it," "Everything will wear off," and "It will be all right." I needed more than conversation. I was no longer a beginner, though not an older member. I was just stuck in the middle, and I wasn't very happy.

Then one of our home group members, someone I really respected, was asked to be the chairman. He agreed on the condition that the group would go through the Steps in order each week, starting with Step One, and so on. When a new person came into the group we would continue with the Steps, but the new person would be properly sponsored and brought up to speed.

This is when I started to take a look at these twelve wonderful Steps, and my whole life began to really change.*

---

*The Twelve Steps of AA are taken from *Alcoholics Anonymous*, 4th ed., published by AA World Services, Inc., New York, NY, 59–60.

STEP ONE *"We admitted we were powerless over alcohol—that our lives had become unmanageable."*

Although I had been an AA member for more than a year, it wasn't until I had gone through the Steps with the group that I fully took Step One. With my history, I hadn't had much difficulty with the idea of being powerless over alcohol. But I had never really looked at the unmanageability part of the Step. Now I could acknowledge that my life, mainly as it related to finances, seemed unmanageable, because I owed a lot of money when I came into AA. For example, the last fight I had, which landed me in the hospital, was over a poker game where I lost quite a bit.

I learned in AA that my financial situation, like many of my other problems, was mostly a result of my ego and my "Big Shot-ism." This is also what made me a liar and a cheat. I needed to get honest about the unmanageability in all of my life; then I could take Step Two.

STEP TWO *"Came to believe that a Power greater than ourselves could restore us to sanity."*

This Step was a pretty difficult one for me because, while I had come from a spiritual home, I had lost all faith during my drinking years. When I came to AA I didn't know what to do about this spirituality stuff. Then they talked about this sanity bit. I thought that being restored to sanity was only for people who had been insane, people who had been in a mental hospital. But I never was in a mental hospital, so how could I relate to this Step?

Then one of my close AA friends took me aside and said, "Think about all those things that you've done, not just while you were drinking but while you were sober. Think of all the insane thoughts, all of your negative thoughts, and you'll see that your thinking was insane." I did exactly what he said, and I was able to move on to Step Three.

STEP THREE *"Made a decision to turn our will and our lives over to the care of God* as we understood Him.*"*

All my life I had difficulty making decisions, because I was always running away from my responsibilities. In Step One I admitted that my life was unmanageable; then in Step Two I discovered who the manager was. Now in Step Three I needed to turn things over to this manager that I chose to call God. My sponsor helped me with this Step by pointing out that all I really needed to do here was make a decision. That's all. I also learned that this Step was asking me only to turn my will and my life over to the God of *my own* understanding. This helped me, because it didn't matter if *you* understood him; all that mattered was my own personal understanding of God and whatever I thought was okay.

STEP FOUR *"Made a searching and fearless moral inventory of ourselves."*

In my company, taking an inventory means reviewing and then writing down everything we have in stock. It's pretty standard business procedure. So when we are talking about the biggest business of all—this business of living a sober life—why is it that so many of us refuse to write it down? We refuse to put pencil to paper. Some simply say, "I can't do that." Over many years of working with people in the program, I've noticed that the toughest part of this Step is getting the pencil and paper.

For example, I have been privileged to be the institutional chairman for our providence. This allows me to work the Twelve Steps with a lot of inmates. When we come to Step Four with these men, we give them a pencil and paper, just in case they should tell us that they couldn't find any. They take their inventory within the prison.

Of course, when I did Step Four myself, I felt there was nothing wrong with me. Then I was told to take my paper, and on the top of the front page I needed to write in big letters,

"NOTHING WRONG WITH ME," and under that write, "I'm a liar!" This would be a good start.

Here's a formula that was given to me for taking Step Four: pick out the person you dislike most in this world, someone you really hate, and begin writing about that person. List all the reasons you don't like them. Write down everything that you dislike about this person. Be honest and write with a vengeance. When you're all done, write *your* name at the top. You will see that you've taken your Step Four.

STEP FIVE *"Admitted to God, to ourselves, and to another human being the exact nature of our wrongs."*

Before proceeding with this Step, we must be sure we've completed an honest and thorough Step Four. When we take a proper Step Four and admit to ourselves and to God the exact nature of our wrongs, then Step Five is simple—all we have to do is go and share it with somebody else. Sometimes I'll hear a newcomer tell another AA member, "I think I need to do my Fifth Step." When the reply the newcomer hears is "Take it easy" and "No hurry," it's likely that the person answering has not done his or her own Fifth Step.

In my own case, I found a little old preacher and sat him down. I thought I'd shake him up a bit with my story. He listened and then shared some things from his own story that almost shook me up. This Step frees us from our drunken shackle and enables us to clean up our side of the street.

STEP SIX *"Were entirely ready to have God remove all these defects of character."*

In 1965 I received a letter from the General Service Office in New York asking me to speak at AA's thirtieth anniversary celebration to be held in Toronto, Canada. I was most honored, but then taken aback when they requested that I speak on Step Six. I asked myself, "Why would they ask me to speak on Step Six? What could I possibility say about this Step?"

Then I picked up my *Twelve Steps and Twelve Traditions* book, turned to Step Six (page 63), and right at the top of the page it said, "This is the step that separates the men from the boys." This Step suggests that I be "entirely" ready to have God remove all my defects of character. In Steps Four and Five all I had done was list and admit my defects, but in Step Six I had to be entirely ready to have them removed. Perhaps I hadn't yet taken this Step because I was afraid of becoming too good too fast or becoming a saint. I've been at this thing for a long time now, and I haven't met any saints yet, not even in Al-Anon.

STEP SEVEN *"Humbly asked Him to remove our shortcomings."*

I love this Step because it is where I learned to get down on my knees. I was one of those guys who would travel around and tell people to pray: Pray while you're driving to work. Pray while you're waiting in line. Pray while riding in a plane or train, or driving down the road. I gave many suggestions on how and where to pray. But I never told anyone to pray by getting down on their knees, because I had never done so myself.

Chi W. is a dear friend I met while in New York. We were delegates to the General Service Conference together. He told a story of how after he came out of prison, he had these high-top boots. While getting ready for bed one night, he mistakenly kicked the boots under his bed. The next morning he had to get down on his knees to find them, and the thought came that while he was down there maybe he should say a few words. So every night since, he's kicked his boots under the bed.

Now I don't wear boots, but after hearing Chi's story I went home and began putting my shoes under the bed so that in the morning I would be reminded to get down on my knees to pray. This was how I began to do this Step, by getting humble and getting on my knees.

STEP EIGHT *"Made a list of all persons we had harmed, and became willing to make amends to them all."*

In Step Eight I was told to make another list of all the people I had harmed and to be willing to make amends to all of them. All this Step asked me to do was to make a list and become willing. Often I'll hear somebody say, "Why should I make a list?" Well, I've seen too many people refuse to make that list and go out and get drunk; that's one reason.

STEP NINE *"Made direct amends to such people wherever possible, except when to do so would injure them or others."*

This is probably the single most important thing I have ever done in my life. My town is small, and going from one end of town to the other was nearly impossible for me, because I had to duck and hide from so many people I had hurt or owed money to.

It wasn't so difficult to make amends by paying back money, because if I didn't do that I would have gone to jail. So I don't really deserve any credit for paying back my financial debts—I really had no other option. The amends that were the hardest to make were to those people who didn't know that I had harmed them. I faced people, explained what I had done, and apologized for my behavior when they weren't even aware of my wrongs. Those were the tough ones.

Then, of course, there were the amends that I needed to make in my own home, with my family. My first attempts at these amends were failures, because by then I had begun working at a good job and earning good money. My thinking was that somehow I could buy my way back into their hearts, when all they wanted was for me to be sober and bring them home a bit of love. They didn't want the many "things" that I bought them; they just wanted some love. I finally learned how to offer my family the unconditional love I found in the rooms of AA.

STEP TEN *"Continued to take personal inventory and when we were wrong promptly admitted it."*

This is the Step that has allowed me to come back into the program without having left it. Let me explain. After I had been sober in the program for ten years, I was working for the wealthiest man in my community. I wanted to be as rich as he was, and as I tried to gain this wealth, which I never did, I became spiritually poor.

During that time I had become complacent with the AA program and had developed an inflated ego with a bad case of "Big Shot-ism." I still attended meetings, but with the attitude of "look at me" and "you're all lucky to have me around." The strange thing about being conceited is that it makes everyone around you sick. My self-centeredness had returned, as had my ego and pride.

I managed five stores for my employer, but he recognized that the business wasn't big enough for me and my ego and that one of us had to go. So he let me go. I thought his business would likely fail within a few months without me. Of course that never happened.

After losing this job, my cousin, another sober AA member, called and told me that she was coming to town from the West Coast. I had last spoken with her about six months earlier and had bragged about how wonderful I was and how successful I had become. Now, even with my life crumbling, I still wanted to make an impression on her. Thank God I didn't drink with the attitude I had!

As I prepared to leave town for a weekend AA roundup, I purchased a new suit, always wanting to look my best. Then I stopped in to see my cousin and asked her how I looked. She looked at me and said some words that changed my life: "You look real good on the outside, but how are you *really* on the inside?" I don't recall if anything else was said that day. I left with another AA member and headed to the roundup, which was several hours away. That entire drive and for the next two days, I couldn't get her words out of my head. How was I *really* on the inside? I spent the entire weekend trying to figure out what I was going to do. Then I did the Tenth Step.

That's when I decided to go back into business, but this time I was going to put the principles of AA to work in my life. I became very active in AA service again, attending meetings, sponsoring people, and getting my priorities in order. I finally learned that when I was having problems, I needed to throw myself into working with other people, and that is what I did.

STEP ELEVEN *"Sought through prayer and meditation to improve our conscious contact with God as we understood Him, praying only for knowledge of His will for us and the power to carry that out."*

When it comes to the Eleventh Step in *Twelve Steps and Twelve Traditions,* the discussion focuses on appreciation, gratitude, and complacency. I wonder how many of us are as grateful as we say we are, how many of us really appreciate Alcoholics Anonymous for what it has done for us, and how many of us just get a little complacent at times. Even when this does happen, the Eleventh Step gives us the opportunity to meditate, pray, and gain a more "conscious contact with God as we understand Him, praying only for the knowledge of His will for us and the power to carry that out." It's so wonderful that we can talk about these things together, about prayer and meditation and about our contact with God. What's so amazing is that we gain this opportunity by doing the previous ten Steps.

The Eleventh Step has taught me many things. Each day I go into a special room in my house to read, meditate, and pray. I like to read from my Big Book and other books that are meaningful to me. One day during my morning prayer time my young granddaughter who was visiting wanted to come into the room. My wife told her I was busy and not to disturb me. She said, "Well, I have something to tell him."

I could hear this going on through the door, so I opened it and invited her in. I put her up on my knee and started to explain what I was doing. When I concluded, I looked down at this beautiful little girl and asked her what it was that she wanted to tell me. She looked up at me with a smile and said, "I just wanted to tell you that I love you." I was able to tell her that I loved her very much too. This may not mean anything to you but it does to me. You see, before I came into AA, I had lost the capacity to accept love and I had no ability to give it. This is why I'm so grateful for Step Eleven.

STEP TWELVE *"Having had a spiritual awakening as the result of these steps, we tried to carry this message to alcoholics, and to practice these principles in all our affairs."*

How often a newcomer will ask, "How do we get a spiritual awakening?" The only way that I know is through these Steps. It took me some time before I understood that the spiritual awakening was a personality change. I learned that this awakening became possible for me through working the previous eleven Steps in sequence. Then I was to try to carry this message to other alcoholics. How often we fail to take time to call on somebody and take them to a meeting. When the phone rings and it's a Twelve Step call do I ask, "Who is it?" instead of asking, "Where is it?" They certainly didn't ask who it was when they came to see me in my time of need, and I'll be forever grateful.

Here is a story that I always enjoy telling while I'm traveling around because I feel it's so significant. It's a story of a young AA member. One day while talking to an older member, he said he was going to quit; the older member asked him why. He said, "When I came to AA, they told me that there were no dues and no fees. They told me that I didn't have to do anything except come to meetings. Now they want me to send money off to the General Service Office. They want me to kick in some money for somebody's birthday. They want me to go sit at some hospital. They want me to go out on Twelve Step calls. I'm getting sick and tired of all this and I think I'm gonna quit."

The older member said, "You know, son, I don't blame you, because your story reminds me of my own story. When my wife and I were quite young, we were blessed with a bouncing baby boy, and although somebody told us that three could live as cheaply as two, from the moment he was born he started to cost me money. My wife had to stay in the hospital and I took the baby home. I had to hire nurses to look after my wife and a housekeeper to look after the boy. Every time I went downtown they asked me to bring something back for that boy. He needed a tricycle, then in public school he needed a bicycle, then he needed other things like clothes for sports. I was like you; I was getting sick and tired of it.

"Finally he went into high school and the bicycle wasn't good enough; he needed a motorcycle. Then he needed an old car and extra money to take girls out. He needed money to go away to camp in the summer, and I was like you, I felt like quitting. I didn't, but then, in his final year of high school, that boy of ours died and he hasn't cost me a penny since."

I believe that this story is something worth thinking about. AA or Al-Anon could slide by the wayside if its members become complacent and stop practicing these principles.

We need to take the principles that we have learned through the Twelve Steps and practice them. Starting with Step One and going through Step Twelve. I was told that "rarely have we seen a person fail who has thoroughly followed our path." This has been my experience with the Steps, and I'm so grateful for them. If you're having trouble with the Steps, I would suggest that you take the *Twelve Steps and Twelve Traditions* book out and read pages 106 to 125, as I was told to. Once we have discovered sobriety, we must then give it away.

There is another story I would like to share. In Palestine

there are two seas. One is the Sea of Galilee, and all around this sea it is beautiful. There are many fish in the sea, children play there, the trees are beautiful, and the sand is nice. Into this wonderful sea flows the river Jordan. Nearby, there is another sea, but there are no fish in this sea, no boats, no children playing, no trees or flowers. Into this sea also flows the river Jordan. What is the difference? The river flows into the Sea of Galilee and flows right through and then is given away. But in the other sea the water flows in and stays there; it is the Dead Sea. I hope that we can all become more like the Sea of Galilee by giving this program away. That's the only way we can keep this wonderful program alive in our own lives.

I've enjoyed many privileges and opportunities through the years as an AA member, including being able to travel and share at conferences and roundups. I was able to serve as a delegate and finally a trustee to the General Service Conference. I was privileged to know Bill W., AA's cofounder. He was a remarkable man. My very best memory of Bill was in Miami at the International Convention held in 1970. Bill was hospitalized at the time, and my dear friend Wesley P. and I went to the hospital to visit him. Later, Bill traveled by ambulance to the hall and addressed the fellowship for the last time. Right up to the end, even as sick as he was, he stood there and continued to give of himself. I never saw Bill after that.

An earlier time, I was traveling by train after the Long Beach International Convention in 1960, and Bill was on the same train. We were standing there talking, and Bill asked if I had ever met Ebby, whom he always considered his sponsor. I told him I hadn't but really looked forward to meeting him one day. Bill said, "Well, walk on up there and introduce yourself; he's just four seats ahead of you." I did and enjoyed a wonderful visit with Ebby; I'm grateful I was able to meet him.

One of the most memorable events in my life was a phone call I received from the GSO in New York. They had received a copy of a talk I gave in Vancouver, British Columbia, on the Twelve Traditions, and were looking for someone who would be willing to travel to Finland to talk with the groups there about the Traditions. That was an incredible honor; I was very excited. I told my friend Wesley and before I knew it, he and Dr. David A. of Dallas and Willard P. all offered to join me on this trip. They gave me some tips, and we just had a great time. I miss a lot of my friends who are no longer with us.

Even though I suffered a stroke a few years ago and now live in a care center here in Prince Albert, I still get to meetings at least twice a week. I celebrated my fifty-seventh sobriety birthday this past January. A few weeks ago the local group had me speak about my experience as a trustee. I'm able to keep very busy with a wonderful life. On Sundays my daughter picks me up and takes me to breakfast, which lasts half the day. So even now, I'm blessed to have people in my life who I love and who love me.

It's funny now looking back and knowing that I was able to participate in so many things. Every time I spoke at conferences and conventions, I shared stories that helped get me started or helped to get a point across. I'll end with this one; it's a true story. There was a man and his wife living in farm country and growing acres of wheat. Late one afternoon their little boy, who was not yet old enough to walk, crawled into the wheat. By the time the parents noticed that he had disappeared, it was getting dark. They called the authorities, and a search party was formed that searched the fields throughout the cold night. They were unsuccessful. The next morning the army sent in some local troops. They had everyone join hands and spread out along the entire width of the farm and slowly walk through the field. It wasn't long before they found the baby, but unfortunately he had already died from exposure. The father, in his sadness, said, "Why couldn't we have joined hands last night and prevented this from happening?"

I believe that the Traditions of Alcoholics Anonymous give us the chance to join together in unity to keep the fellowship together and to save lives. In closing, I would simply like to ask, "You all look real good on the outside, but how are you *really* on the inside?"

"From Hard Cider at Age Three
to Hard Knocks at Age Thirty-Three"

THE STORY OF CLARA F.

When you're ninety years old and have been sober in Alcoholics Anonymous for more than fifty-seven years, as I have, there's not a debate about this disease that you haven't heard or participated in.

The one debate I've always enjoyed the most was whether people are born alcoholics or whether they simply develop this terrible disease over many years of heavy drinking. Perhaps the reason I enjoy listening to others debate this issue is because I found the answer to it in my life a long, long time ago.

I know I was born an alcoholic. When I tell you my story, I think you will agree with me.

It was the start of the Prohibition era when I made my initial appearance in 1920 as a rather plump little baby girl, born to a potato farmer and his wife in Belding, Michigan. It was a time when those good old suffragettes tried to convince everyone they'd go directly to hell if they struck up a relationship with that infamous John Barleycorn.

Looking back, neither they nor the Volstead Act ever stopped anyone from drinking, even in our house. People like my father and his farmhands just used a little ingenuity. And when you grow potatoes, it's pretty easy—potatoes make real great home brew.

We also had a lot of apple trees on our farm. When we picked them in the fall, my father would store them in a fruit cellar near our barn. That's also where he'd make his hard cider, putting in all the good stuff like sugar and spices.

One day when I was about three and a half, I followed my dad down into that fruit cellar. He had a big gallon jug of hard cider on a bench. He filled a tumbler, saw me standing there looking up at him, and handed me the glass to take a little sip. Instead, I drank the whole thing. He seemed amazed, especially when I only burped a few times and didn't throw up right then and there.

He patted me on the head and left to do some chores. I kept staring at the jug. Then one of the farmhands came into the fruit cellar and poured himself a tumbler of cider. I smiled up at him and said my daddy told me I could have a glass and that I could finish the whole thing. He handed me the glass and again I drank it all down. After he left, another fellow came in and I did the same thing.

After finishing my third big glass of hard cider, I began feeling a little woozy. So I staggered out of the fruit cellar and into the field, tripping and falling down in the rows of potatoes. My father saw me and figured out what I had done. He picked me up, brought me into the house, and he and my mother put me to bed. It was early afternoon and I slept until noon the next day. I think he and my mom were afraid I'd never wake up. When I finally did, I felt so proud of the fact that I could drink so much hard cider and not get sick. For years after that I would frequently brag about my alcohol intake.

That incident and many that followed convinced me I was born an alcoholic. Whenever I drank, I always wanted more. As I said, my father would also make home brew from his potatoes. He'd brew it in our basement using these metal tanks that had a faucet on the bottom. I'd watch him pump it up and pour it out just like bartenders do in a tavern. Soon I was sneaking down into the basement and doing it myself.

We stored a lot of things in the basement, but for some reason my mother was afraid to go down there. I wasn't, so she'd send me down to fetch whatever she needed. Sometimes she'd ask why it took me so long to get it. I never let anybody know I was sneaking beer every time I went into the basement.

As I grew up, my desire to drink continued, but the opportunity to drink a whole lot was rare until I got into high school and began going to parties and dances. I guess I was around fifteen or sixteen years old when I first started attending these barn dances at a nearby farm. I was a rather chubby little gal at that time and felt shy and awkward about my weight. Some kids would tease me, so I would hang back and watch everyone else dance, using the excuse that I didn't know how. Then one night some boys brought a whole lot of beer to the dance. One fellow I knew who was always nice to me said I could have some beer if I wanted. Well, I had more than some and before I knew it, I was out on the dance floor with this fellow dancing like a whiz.

That's when I discovered how alcohol could enable me to do things I had always been too shy and afraid to try. It opened up a whole new world for this shy, overweight little gal.

One day I went with some friends to a resort on Kirkon Lake and met a real nice guy—kind of straight-laced but very sweet. We started dating and then got engaged. By this time I loved going out and having a good time dancing and partying and always drinking a little too much. I could see it was bothering my fiancé. One night he tells me he won't go out with me anymore if I continue to drink so much and get drunk too often. I really liked him so I cut back on my drinking just to please him. But it didn't please me.

Around the same time, World War II broke out, and he was called into the service and sent overseas. By now I had graduated from high school and had gotten a job at a local manufacturer of children's clothing. I met a bunch of people there who liked to go fishing on weekends. Many of them were heavy drinkers, so I fit right in. One of the real good drinkers in the group was a fellow named Cleo. We started going out together, fell in love, and decided to get married. I was still engaged to my boyfriend overseas, so I had to write him a "Dear John" letter.

I felt very guilty about doing it, so I had quite a few drinks before I took pen in hand. That's the way I used to handle my guilt—drink it away. I don't know about you, but when I got drunk, I could always find a way to justify my actions.

Cleo and I got married in 1944 and started a family right away. We soon had two girls and two boys, all who turned out to be very lovely and very kind people despite being raised by alcoholic parents. I did have the good sense, however, not to drink when I was pregnant. Actually, I think it was more of God helping me do the right thing than any common sense of my own, because I would start pouring down the booze again not long after giving birth.

There were many times when I wasn't much of a mother, too drunk to help my children with their schoolwork and sometimes shaming them in front of their friends. They wouldn't know what kind of condition they would find me in when they came home from school. And then there was the screaming and shouting every time their father and I would get into a drunken argument. They'd go into their rooms and close the door, hoping nothing real bad would happen.

I rarely looked at myself and my own drinking. I always focused on Cleo, who got very bad toward the end. He was spending so much money on alcohol that I had to go to work at a hardware store to help support the family. There I was, struggling out of bed in the morning with a hangover, trying to get the kids ready for school, and going to work with the shakes until lunch break and a few drinks. Then I'd go home, make dinner, and drink myself to sleep. It wasn't the kind of life I had hoped for.

Then my husband started getting physically abusive. Although my smart mouth would often egg him on, I still wasn't going to stand for it. I thought about getting a divorce, but I didn't make enough money to support four children and our home. I now had every excuse in the world to drink, but I hated myself every time I did. I just didn't know what to do. That's when God stepped in once again.

My husband got arrested for drunken driving and was thrown into jail. The only lawyer he knew to call for help was an old drinking buddy he hadn't seen in several years. My husband was still trying to hang on to a pretty good job, and he needed to keep his driver's license for work. His old buddy said he knew the judge and could probably get the charge reduced to reckless driving on one condition—that my husband join a program called Alcoholics Anonymous. Little did Cleo know at the time that his old lawyer buddy had been sober in AA himself for almost two years.

When Cleo came home and told me he was going to a meeting of Alcoholics Anonymous, I was both surprised and confused. I had never heard of AA, so I didn't know what he was talking about. He explained that it was a place that helped people get sober and stay sober and that because he was between a rock and a hard place, he decided to give it a try.

Now I can't tell you whether my next thought came because I wanted to be a loving and supporting wife or because deep down I knew I had a serious drinking problem myself. I think it was the latter. Anyway, I told my husband I would like to go with him to see what this AA thing was all about.

The next night we went together to our first AA meeting

in Belding, Michigan. That was on September 8, 1953—and neither one of us ever had a drink since that day.

There were no women at the meeting back then and only about a dozen or so men. None of them said anything about my being there, since they assumed I had only come along to support my husband. As soon as I heard some of those men speak, I began comparing myself to their terribly painful and humiliating stories and wondered why I had come in the first place. Yes, I could identify a bit with some of their feelings, but not with some of their awfully low "bottoms."

When we got home that night, I thought about drinking. While I was still very confused, that feeling inside that told me I had a serious problem with alcohol would not go away. So I said a prayer and went to bed without having a drink. It had been a long time since that happened, so I did have trouble falling asleep.

A few weeks later we were invited to an AA meeting with a potluck supper in Greenville. It turned out to be the most important AA meeting I ever made in my whole life. An old-timer named Chi W., who has long since passed away, spoke that night. I sat there thinking, "Who told him all those things about me?" I hung on to his every word because I identified with the way he described my disease of alcoholism, how I had always denied it, how it had affected my life, and how it would only get worse if I kept on drinking. I knew now that I was definitely powerless over alcohol.

When I went back to the next meeting in Belding and announced that I was an alcoholic and wanted to join the group, they almost had apoplexy. I could tell they didn't want me there simply because I was a woman. They said they would have to vote to see if I could join. I got a little miffed and said I didn't care how their vote came out—I was joining the group whether they liked it or not because I wanted to stay sober. On the way home, Cleo said he was proud of me.

So my AA life began. My husband and I made a lot of

meetings together all over the county. We also read AA's Big Book and the Twelve Steps together at home. My whole life began to change, along with my relationship with my children and our family and friends and especially with Cleo. We began to love each other again like we did when we first met. I think even more.

It was five years before another woman came into our Belding AA group. Shortly after, a third one joined. We all drew very close, both the men and the women. It became like one big family, each one helping to keep the other one sober.

I was sober about two years when I was out in the woods with my husband one day hunting deer. We had always loved to hunt and fish, but as our alcoholism progressed, we seldom went anymore. Now that we were sober, we were enjoying it more than ever. As we headed back to our car, I suddenly stumbled and fell to the ground. Cleo tried to help me up, but I could hardly move and had difficulty breathing. He carried me to the car and drove directly to the hospital.

I was diagnosed with a sudden onset of a severe form of polio. My lungs, throat, hands, and legs were paralyzed, and they didn't expect me to live. I was hospitalized for many months. During my convalescence, I kept turning my life and my will over to the care of God and using the Serenity Prayer during those most fearful of times. It was only through the grace of God and the prayers of my husband, children, and many friends that I finally did pull through. I guess God still had more work for me to do. The only lasting effect I have is trouble swallowing cold things, but what a minor concern after you've been given back your life.

About a year later, one of my daughters also got polio. Thank God it wasn't nearly as severe and left her with no aftereffects. I was so grateful to be sober during her illness and to be at her bedside to help nurse her back to health. Once again it was my Higher Power giving me the chance to make amends.

Both my husband and I sponsored quite a few people over the years. Sometimes we'd bring them home and help them get back on their feet physically. Cleo was a very generous man, often putting some of those alcoholics up in rooming houses and paying their rent until they could get a job. We'd often bring some of the tougher cases to detoxes in Lansing, Detroit, and Muskegon. Believe it or not, after leaving them at the hospital, we would learn that some of them had beat us back to Belding. What a terribly insidious and powerful disease this is. But through it all, by trying to carry the message to others, Cleo and I grew stronger in sobriety and closer as a couple.

While my husband was always kind and generous to the men he sponsored, I think I was much tougher on the women I sponsored and still am. If I spotted them on the street, I'd follow them around to see where they were going. I remember one day I was driving through town and saw this girl I sponsored come out of a store with a six-pack of beer. I pulled the car over and demanded she get in. As we drove across a bridge on our way to a meeting a few miles away, I grabbed the beer from her and tossed it out the window into the river below. I think it made an impression on her because she stayed sober.

Another time I learned some guy in another group was hitting on a lady I sponsored. She was fairly new and quite vulnerable when it came to sex. I found this guy at a meeting one night, backed him up against a wall, and shouted so loud that the whole room could hear me: "I sponsor that lady and you better leave her alone or you'll answer to me!" He left her alone.

When it comes to sex, or what people in the program call "Thirteenth Stepping," I always put the women I sponsor on notice. I tell them that an affair in early sobriety, particularly with another sick guy in the fellowship, can only lead to emotional disaster and another drink. I also tell them that sometimes they bring it on themselves by the way they dress and act—that even old-timers like to look up short skirts and down loose blouses, so don't wear them.

I firmly believe that every woman who really wants to stay sober and avoid being hit on should dress like a lady. I sometimes feel there isn't enough respect for each other in AA these days—with both men and women. We come here to clean up both inside and outside and to lead a spiritual life. After all, the Big Book tells us that our sobriety is dependent on our spiritual condition.

In 1975, my husband retired and we decided to move to a warmer climate. We bought a place in Tavares, Florida, where we had some AA friends. We stayed just as active in the program there as we had been in Belding.

Shortly after we moved, Cleo began to feel tired and sluggish, so he went to see a doctor. He was diagnosed with heart disease and put on medication. He did quite well for the next ten years until he had his first heart attack. While he recovered, he was never quite the same. He died in 1987 from a second heart attack. We had been married more than forty-four years.

Thank God I had the AA program and so many good friends to support me after my husband's death. There was one particular couple Cleo and I were very close to who helped me through my grief. The man, Jim, had been Cleo's closest friend and fishing buddy. Well, about a year later, his wife also passed away and Jim and I soon found ourselves going out to dinner, spending time together, and making a lot of AA meetings together. In 1990 we got married and enjoyed the next twelve years or so as a happy AA couple.

Jim passed away in 2003, and I decided to move back to Belding to be closer to my children. I wasn't getting any younger and wasn't always feeling as chipper as I'd like to.

Since I returned, I've continued to focus on the three important things that keep me happy, joyous, and free. The first is working and living the AA program to the best of my ability.

The second thing is to make as many meetings as I can, so I can be there when others may need my help. And the third is sponsoring women in the fellowship, something that keeps my heart happy and my love strong. If I continue to do these things, then I can stay not only a sober woman but also a sober mother to my children, a sober grandmother to my fifteen grandchildren, and a sober great grandmother to my great grandchild.

I have so much to be grateful for in my life, and it's all the result of being sober in AA. After suffering polio and living through many surgeries over the years, I'm so fortunate to be alive and still have the opportunity to carry the message of recovery to others. Some of my friends and sponsees call me the bionic woman. I have a pacemaker, two artificial knees, and an artificial shoulder. I've had back surgery, no movement in one arm, and difficulty swallowing. But I'm in God's hands and have nothing to worry about.

I've experienced much during my fifty-seven years of sobriety—seeing a woman I sponsor relapse and throw boiling water on her husband as they argued, another conk her husband over the head with a rolling pin because he wouldn't give her any money to drink, and still another try to run over her drunken husband with her car because she caught him cheating on her. All three of these ladies are now sober in AA.

Ours is a program of miracles, a program of hope and joy, a fellowship that surrounds us with loving support. Thank God I'm only ninety and still have so much time ahead of me to enjoy life in Alcoholics Anonymous.

"There was a time when I was willing to drive fifty miles to talk but unwilling to go one mile to listen. Thank God that ego trip is over."

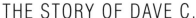

THE STORY OF DAVE C.

When it came to my alcoholism, my mother had always been my greatest enabler. Then one day, shortly after I turned twenty-nine, she gave me the greatest gift she had ever given me. She cut me out of her life.

It was August 1957. I staggered up to her front door after another one of my many long bouts with booze. I had once again embarrassed my family and shamed and devastated this wonderful woman who tried to believe in me for so many years despite my lies and broken promises. She saw me coming. Before I could knock, she opened the door and stared at me. Tears ran down her cheeks, her face revolted at the sight of me, and the words she uttered were filled with pain and hopelessness.

"You are no longer my son," she said. "You are not in my life any longer. I wish you well and I will pray for you, but please don't call me or come around here ever again." Then she closed the door.

A month later I got sober and have never had a drink or a mood-altering drug since.

My father was also an alcoholic, and my parents divorced when I was twelve. Left to raise us alone, my mother almost loved me to death. She was the one who really raised me, clothed me, and gave me an education. She did the same thing for my two younger sisters, but they never caused her the problems and heartache that I did.

As I say, I think she tried to make up for my father leaving, because we had been close growing up. My father would take me hunting and fishing when he was sober, but then his drinking got worse and worse. He owned a dry goods business and lost it all. He died in a drunken automobile wreck at the age of fifty-four. My mother, who never remarried, died at the age of eighty-two after seeing me sober for many years, thank God.

I was born in Henderson, North Carolina, on November 3, 1927, but spent most of my childhood in Roanoke Rapids. I did so well in high school that they advanced me a year. I entered High Point University at the age of sixteen, where I majored in math and engineering—and drinking.

At the time, guys were just returning from World War II and entering college on the GI Bill. And they all knew how to drink. So I began to do what the big boys were doing, and I worked real hard at it.

They would talk about the pleasure that comes from drinking. I didn't know what the heck they were talking about because I was always throwing up, especially on wine, which would also give me a headache for days. So one day I asked one of these ex-GIs, "When does that pleasure from drinking you're always talking about finally come?" He grinned and said, "Dave, if you remember, there's a little pause in between the time you take the drink and the time when you throw up.

It's during that pause when the pleasure comes." So I continued working at it and sure enough, the pleasure finally started coming—along with the beginning of my troubles.

My drinking really picked up when I joined a fraternity. To show you how much we drank at that frat house, six of us members eventually wound up in Alcoholics Anonymous.

In between my studies and my drinking, I also played basketball and got to know the game quite well. So when I finished college, I took a job as a high school basketball coach and teacher. Looking back, I realize I did it mainly for the glory and adulation that coaching often brings. I had what we call in AA a big, fat alcoholic ego.

But I became quite successful in this field, getting hired by larger and larger high schools as a professional basketball coach. The more successful I became, the more I drank. And the more I drank, the more trouble I found—including marrying a girl I'd known for only two weeks and marrying her against my mother's wishes. The marriage didn't last.

After about six years of coaching ball and drinking every time I got the chance, my troubles grew more serious. I was now drinking in the mornings and was plastered by nightfall. For the first time, the school principal approached me about my drinking. I not only denied I had a problem, but told him I resented his accusations. Deep down, however, I knew the truth . . . and also knew I was on shaky ground.

Although I was a good basketball coach and teacher, I finally got fired from that very large and prominent school over a "misunderstanding" related to the girls' basketball team. It seems the coach of the girls' team was suddenly called up for military service, and I was asked to take over the team in addition to my other duties.

By now I was going to these basketball games half soused up, drinking vodka for breakfast and lunch. Of course I believed that nobody could smell vodka or notice the way I walked—very loose with good fluid movement. That was the way I showed up the first night I had to coach one of the girls' basketball games.

I gathered them together in a huddle to give them instructions and a pep talk. Then, without thinking, as we broke the huddle I patted a few of them on the rear just like I always did with the boys. Some of the parents came tearing down from the stands and we had one helluva mess before the ball game even started.

You can guess what happened. The school board met the next morning, and I was given my walking papers, though they were nice enough to let me resign. Of course, my drinking played a major part in this mess. So I moved to another school farther east, and then another one a little bit farther east. My drinking seemed to keep me moving east.

I finally wound up at the rock-bottom of schools and didn't last six months. The wife I had known for only two weeks before marrying had had enough. She left for parts unknown. And my mother—well, she had been trying to help me all along, encouraging me, chiding me, sending me money. Now she began a whole new effort. While there were no such things as treatment centers back then, there were drying-out places. She paid my way into such places in Connecticut, New Jersey, and Virginia for my "nervous breakdowns."

These places tapered you off, which I actually began to enjoy, but never fully completed the process. Still, I enjoyed trying and began looking forward to my stays there. In between, my mother sent me to doctors, psychologists, psychiatrists, and even ministers for help. Nothing seemed to work.

As I look back now, everybody told me what the problem was, but nobody gave me a solution. And my mother was spending a lot of money trying to keep me sober. For a brief period I did stay dry. I wouldn't call it sobriety; I just didn't drink. I got another teaching and coaching job but was soon drinking again and facing even more trouble than before.

I found myself getting up at four or five in the morning

and having a drink to stop the shakes. Then I'd get dressed and go to school, praying for three o'clock to come, when I'd have a break to drink before basketball practice. I had booze hidden in the gymnasium, as well as in my car, so I could stop the shakes while driving back to town, where I'd start drinking all over again.

This went on for a few months until the principal stopped me in the hall one day and said very calmly, "We don't need you anymore." There was no conference. He didn't call me into his office to talk about it. He simply asked for my keys to the school and walked away.

I now knew that I had crossed that invisible line we speak of in Alcoholics Anonymous. While I didn't actually know about the line back then, I knew I had become an alcoholic who, once he took a drink, could no longer guarantee his behavior.

While I had experienced blackouts before, they were never prolonged. The two weeks after I left the school that day are missing from my memory. I don't know where I went, but I woke up in jail in the city where I was living. Apparently, I had already been there for a few days. A man was staring at me through my cell door. He was the county health doctor, and he said, "Your mother has come down here and straightened out the mess you've created. Now we're going to send you to a place where they can cure you."

Now at that time, the word "cure" didn't quite register. I thought he was talking about sending me back to one of those places where I used to taper off, where I'd sit in a lawn chair under an umbrella and sip, sip, sip as I tapered. But this doctor didn't mean that at all. He meant our state insane asylum called Dix Hill. That's where he was sending me to be cured.

I've often said since then, kidding of course, that, "I found my thrill on Dix Hill." I was twenty-seven at the time and so help me God, as long as I draw a sober breath, I never want to forget my first trip to Dix Hill. They put me in the Inebriate Ward for the first few days. I didn't know what it meant but it sounded okay until I discovered that the people in that ward chased squirrels most of the time. They would run up and down the walls—the squirrels, that is. I figured when in Rome do as the Romans do. So I chased squirrels, too, and got pretty darn good at it. I never caught one, but I think I came close a few times.

I'd been in there almost two weeks when they suddenly moved me into a ward called Skid Row. That's where they kept all the rummies who were still shaking it off and trying to get their legs to obey orders. I was tossed into a padded cell in the basement where they took away all my clothes and let me have my running fits. Some days later when I got through my running fits, they returned my clothes and let me walk up and down the corridor, day in and day out. I began wondering what the heck I was doing here, because everybody was so much older and looked so much sicker.

I remember one night watching some older gentlemen playing poker, using matchsticks for chips. I've never forgotten them nor the desperate looks on their faces. They were talking about the reason they were in an insane asylum. One man said, "I'm here because my wife wanted to get rid of me." I remember identifying with that comment, thinking that my mother was finally trying to get rid of me, too. She had tried everything she knew to do, spent big money doing it, and had finally reached the end of her rope.

And then I heard another man say, "I'm here because I'm an alcoholic." That's when I thought about my father, who was also an alcoholic, and I remembered that old saying, "Like father, like son." Then I thought, no, I'm too young to be a real alcoholic. You have to be old like these guys.

The very first time I heard anything about Alcoholics Anonymous was in Dix Hill. Every Sunday afternoon people from Raleigh would come in and hold an AA meeting. I'd go just to drink the coffee and eat the doughnuts and sit in the back row raising hell. I'd make fun of the guy standing up there trying to give us the message about the solution to our problem. I was about five years sober before I finally realized a very significant fact. Every Sunday that guy who gave his talk and tried to help us would walk out the front gates and go home. I stayed. You know, alcoholics are kind of slow on picking up on things like that.

When it came time for my release, I didn't have anywhere to go. Once again my mother let her now twenty-eight-year-old son come back home, but she immediately called our family doctor to check me over. He was quite ignorant of my situation. You know how families like to keep secrets about their alcoholics. But the good doctor thought I had a problem with my nerves and prescribed some "tablets." Now, I don't know anything about drugs, but I did learn a lot about "tablets."

I began taking them like popcorn and became loose as a goose. I was running around with the old crowd from school. They would drink and I would take my medicine . . . and stay loose as a goose most of the time.

I'd been home about nine weeks when my old friends passed around a bottle one night and I decided to have a swig. Today, as a result of this program, I know that the compulsion we speak of quickly set in. I took another drink and then another. To make a long story short, I wound up back in Dix Hill, the place I swore I'd never return to—but I returned five more times in six months. I'd become a raging alcoholic and didn't know it.

During my last time at Dix Hill, they put me in the nut part of the bughouse instead of the drying-out part. There's a distinct difference. I found out about being tied down to a bed and how you live better electrically. Yes, I found out about that, too.

I wish I could say I got sober in Dix Hill and stayed that way. But my ride into alcoholic oblivion didn't end there. I was one of those people who had to be beat to my knees before I could see myself. And that's the thing I don't understand about this disease, even today with more than fifty years of sobriety. In spite of working with a whole lot of newcomers and others in the AA program, I do not understand why alcoholics cannot see themselves as they really are in their worst moments. This was the thing that almost killed me—that I just could not see myself.

After some time, I was transferred to the drying-out ward. I befriended two other drunks who decided they were going to break out of the asylum. So I joined them, and we escaped with the cops right on our tail. Somehow we eluded them and wound up in this fleabag hotel all rummied up, watching television. The news came on about three insane inmates escaping from Dix Hill, and we wondered who the heck they were talking about. That's how sick we were.

I borrowed some money from an old friend of my mother's so I could get back to my hometown and clean up a bit. That's when I tried to contact my mother and learned that she had a nervous breakdown and was in a hospital in Richmond, Virginia. I was so filled with guilt, I started drinking all over again.

My sisters called a family meeting to discuss what should be done about me. They decided to pool together a bunch of money and give it to me, provided I promised to go far, far away and leave my mother alone. I told them I'd go way out to the West Coast. Well, I didn't get quite that far. I managed to get about four miles away, checked into a little hotel, and partied with my old school buddies until the money ran out. Then in blackouts, I did some things that got me arrested, tried, and convicted. I was sent to prison, where I worked on a chain gang. I found out I had written a number of bad checks against my mother's bank account that the family convinced her not to cover.

The day I was released from prison, I didn't know what to do or where to go. You're taken to the city limits of your hometown and left to fend for yourself. By then my mother had fully recovered from her breakdown so, deeply ashamed and filled with fear, I went to her house and knocked on her back door. My sisters and brothers-in-law were there and told her not to let me in. But one more time my mother stood up for me and said, "That's my boy and he'll stay here tonight whether you all like it or not."

And that's what I did. I stayed at my mother's home that night and for the next four months. She fed me, clothed me, and got me back on my feet. I made a vow not to drink because of her. I'd do it for her. I don't recommend that anyone stop drinking for someone else. It doesn't work.

Things did go better for a while, however. I didn't think I could get a teaching or coaching job in North Carolina, but through an agency in Richmond, Virginia, I got a teaching position in Roanoke, Virginia. It was a fresh start in life. My mother's faith in me was paying off. She gave me money for my trip to Roanoke and rent for a small apartment. When I arrived I was excited, but scared. Little did I know I was about to begin my last drunk.

It's amazing how the mental part of this disease works on you. I thought since I was sober almost five months, one little drink to bolster my confidence wouldn't hurt. I took one . . . and never stopped. I managed to last just five days on my job. This time the school officials actually tried to help me, but without success. They even contacted my mother after I told them I was going home.

That's when my mother gave me the greatest gift she could have given me. She disowned me.

On Sunday, September 11, 1957, I came to lying in a back alley in downtown Roanoke on Skid Row; I was trying to get a drink of liquor down. The thought occurred to me that I was going to die in this back alley from my alcoholism. I had ten pennies in my pocket, a razor and a toothbrush in a little paper bag, and the clothes on my back. That's all I had left. Everything else was gone, including my self-respect. My moment of truth had finally arrived. I didn't want to die all alone on Skid Row. I cried out for help, and God answered my plea.

The only man in the city who knew me on a first-name basis had been looking for me. He was the superintendent of schools. He found me and carried me to his home that morning. He called a man he knew in Alcoholics Anonymous, and that afternoon I was carried to a Twelve Step clubhouse in downtown Roanoke called the Easy Does It Club. That's where I began to shake off my final drunk. I've never had a drink or a drug since.

I met a guy that day who helped me as much as anyone ever had before. They called him Old Man John. He put his arm around me and simply said, "Dave, all you got to do is listen to these people and do what they tell you, and you'll never have to be alone again." Old Man John came to AA when he was seventy-six. He died at eighty-two with six continuous years of sobriety. I will never forget the love and inspiration he gave me at a time in my life when I needed it the most.

I attended my first AA meeting at the clubhouse that night. I don't remember much about it except that after the meeting, strangers kept coming up to me, putting their arms around my shoulder, and saying, "We love you, Dave, and we understand how you feel right now. But you're going to be all right if you stay with us. That's a promise." They convinced me that what Old Man John had said that afternoon was the truth—that I didn't have to be alone ever again.

Three men got me a room at the local YMCA and stayed with me all night long to make sure I'd be okay. Since I couldn't sleep, they took turns talking to me about Alcoholics Anonymous and the gift of sobriety. They also told me that if I got too bad, they were going to get a doctor for me. I shook, but I listened to them until the sun came up. That's when a guy named Clyde said, "You've been so many hours without a drink now, Dave, I think you got a chance of making it today. That how we do it in AA. We don't drink, one day at a time."

That was the first time I ever heard it put that way, and it helped me enormously. That's also when I think I came to believe that this thing called Alcoholics Anonymous could work for me—if I stayed around people like these. Now, more than fifty-three years later, I still need to be around sober AA members. I've seen too many people try to do it another way—they leave us and stop making meetings altogether—and most of them got drunk.

And so that was my beginning in Alcoholics Anonymous. I met my first sponsor the next morning. I didn't have a thing to do with it; he was appointed. He arranged for me to stay in a boarding house with six other men. We each had our own room, and I don't know who paid for my rent and food my first four months in the program. That's the God's honest truth. But that's the love of one alcoholic for another.

I learned much from the six men I roomed with. Today, three of them have passed on, one is still drinking, and two of us remain sober. I told one of them, Charlie P., that I loved him, the first man in AA I ever said that to. I told him because of how much he helped me. And I still love him as a brother, as I do so many of my friends in this wonderful program.

I began this sober journey by doing what I was told to do. I had no job at the time and was filled with fear. But I had good sponsorship and was being led through the Twelve Steps of recovery. I'd been sober a few months when I met my second wife, Sue. She had never seen me drink or drunk, but she went through more hell than my first wife watching me trying to grow up. She wouldn't marry me until I was sober two years—and still trying to grow up. That was in 1960. Sue died from cancer in 1997. I met my present wife, Julie, in the fellowship a year later, and we married soon after that.

I've learned much more from people in AA with much less education than I had. For example, after I was sober awhile I started looking for a job. One night after a meeting, I was speaking with this fellow named Red about my employment problem. Red was a sign painter with a third-grade education. He said, "Dave, it seems to me that if you studied engineering in college, that's what you ought to be doing in life." Heck, nobody had ever explained it that way to me before.

Not long after that, Red and Sue drove me to an interview for an engineering job with Virginia's highway department. It was the second week of December, 1957. The man asked me a lot of questions and, trying to abide by AA's principle of rigorous honesty, I told him the absolute truth. He looked me straight in the eye and said, "Son, if you're willing to help yourself, we're willing to help you, too. When can you go to work?"

I was shocked and scared to death. I blurted out that I had a lot of business to tend to and probably couldn't start until about the first of February. He said that would be fine. When I returned to the car and told Red and Sue what happened, they marched me right back into that man's office and told him I could start working the very next day.

This is how I learned that fear can really slow us down and that we must put our trust in God and the AA program. I had to be led like this in the beginning, by loving friends like Red and Sue and so many others who really loved and cared about me.

As I put more sober days together, I started to feel like an important member of my AA group. I didn't realize that my big ego was still there ready to burst forth until the night the steering committee let me speak from the podium. Instead of simply sharing my own story, I started giving advice to one of the guys from the boarding house who had just gotten drunk again. I thought I could talk him sober. It never occurred to me that even people with years of sobriety have trouble talking to a drunk drunk.

After a few minutes of this egotistical nonsense, I heard someone in "Serenity Row" where all the old-timers gathered say, "Sit down." Not thinking he was speaking to me, I continued rambling on with my advice to this poor guy until the voice from the rear shouted more loudly, "I said to sit down." Someone finally had to come up to the podium and lead me back to my seat. I should have been embarrassed, but with the ego I had at the time there wasn't a chance.

One of my big problems was that I was hanging around people who would tell me, "Take what you think you need and throw away the rest." I didn't realize at the time that I needed everything in the program, just as all alcoholics do. In fact, I got to the point where I'd be willing to drive fifty miles to speak but wouldn't be willing to go one mile to listen. That ego trip ended when my sponsor began teaching me about humility. Thank God my ego didn't get me drunk before then.

In 1960 I moved to Raleigh, North Carolina, where I married Sue and went to work for the North Carolina Highway Department, a job I held until I retired thirty-two years later. I met a man there named Tom B., who became my new sponsor and helped change my life for the better. Tom was a good friend of Bill W.'s and the man who replaced Dr. Bob as a trustee on the old Alcoholic Foundation, the forerunner of AA's World Service Office. He got me more deeply involved in the Twelve Steps and the Big Book. When I'd ask him a question, he'd say, "Read the book, then we'll talk."

Tom also got me involved in AA service work after I once bad-mouthed our General Service Office. He handed me a service manual, told me to read it, and then found me a service job in the program. In 1965 I became my group's GSR (general service representative) and the following year the area committeeman for our North Carolina state committee. Two years later I was elected delegate for Panel 17, and following that I became delegate chairman. That's when I got to know our cofounder Bill W. and discovered he was a human being just like myself and everyone else. I always suggest that everyone get involved in AA service work.

It took nine and a half years for my mother to accept me back in her life. She finally came to know what Alcoholics

Anonymous was all about and how it had saved and changed her son's life. She found it to be, as she often said, "the greatest thing I've ever seen." She lived to see me sober for more than thirty-two years. We drew far closer than ever before and had many wonderful times together right up to her passing. What a great gift God gave me to have this special woman back in my life.

I know without a doubt that the only way for me to hold on to this tremendous gift of sobriety is to commit myself to do four important things. The first is to continue working this program and carrying it to others, just as those three men from the Easy Does It Club back in Roanoke, Virginia, did for me in the fall of 1957. Second, I have to go to meetings because that's where it's at. That's where I hear what I need to hear to help me stay sober, and that's where I share what God wants me to share to help others. Third, I have to live the Twelve Steps each and every day. That's the program of Alcoholics Anonymous, the program that helps me maintain the kind of spirituality I need to stay sober. And four, no matter how things are going in my life, I must hang on to what I believe and keep my faith in my Higher Power, whom I chose to call God.

My sponsor, Tom B., told me many years ago, "Nothing's so bad that it won't get better if you just hang on. Believe in this program and do what the program asks you to do."

Looking back at the past fifty-three years or so, I really believe that yesterday is my experience and tomorrow is my hope. Today is going from one to the other and doing the best I can. As long as I have the privilege to walk with you hand in hand down this happy road to destiny, I also believe that I will be allowed one more day of sobriety. For that is the promise of AA, the promise of God himself—and for that I will be forever grateful.

"From the Fantasy World of Motion Picture Theaters to the Real-Life Drama of Alcoholics Anonymous"

THE STORY OF DON W.

I was born in Sydney, Australia, on January 15, 1929, and from my earliest recollections I was a boy of many moods and emotions—from fear to envy to loneliness. Perhaps this was due to my low self-esteem, which was constantly looking for ways to be propped up.

For example, I remember being the envy of my schoolmates as a youngster when my father managed two local movie theaters in New South Wales. I was able to free-view the week's feature film at the matinee every Saturday afternoon. I recall the day I saw my first color film, *The Wizard of Oz*. In fact, I saw it twice, and it gave me great status with my schoolmates. I was admired by everyone, which really built up my self-esteem.

However, I didn't hold on to this status for long. World War II broke out and changed everything. All the eligible young people joined the armed forces, fuel was rationed (which restricted farmers and families driving into town regularly), and money became tight. As a result, the movie audiences fell off dramatically and my father slid into bankruptcy. All the glamour and attention surrounding me went away. I was no longer the big fish in my small pond. My low self-esteem returned in spades and remained until I eventually found another solution to my problem—alcohol.

My parents, both third-generation Australians, were brought up in rural districts northwest of Sydney. To us three kids our mother was the heart of our family. Our father, on the other hand, was by nature a very private man, becoming even more so following his bankruptcy, which in those days was regarded as somewhat of a disgrace. He spent the rest of his career as an insurance agent. Neither he nor my mother were drinkers, though drinking was in plague proportions on my mother's side of the family.

I think I inherited some of my father's traits. He was a quiet, introverted man who couldn't even talk to his sons about the facts of life or, for that matter, anything intimate. So my brother, John, who was three years older than I, became my sounding board and confidant.

My self-esteem was further challenged by my family's frequent moves. I'd attended five different schools by the time I was sixteen in 1945, preventing any enduring bonding with schoolmates and adding to my feelings of aloneness.

Then a tragedy struck our family four months before the end of the war. My brother, John, who by then was a sergeant front-turret gunner with the Royal Australian Air Force on Liberator bombers based in Darwin, was reported as "missing in action." In those days this meant "killed in action." The news devastated us all and pushed me, at sixteen, even further into myself. Losing my older brother and confidant fed my insecurity and the anger and self-pity that was growing inside of me.

Soon after I finished schooling, I was taken on as a trainee in the accounts office of Sydney's largest commercial laundry and dry cleaning company. It was here that I first began to drink. Three years into the job I started attending night school to study accountancy. I soon found the classes were clashing with my after-work imbibing, so I quit the course—a move that did not impress management. But by now, after-work drinking had become the norm. For some reason, I usually drank with older men, and in a very short time, these men were warning me about not letting my drinking get out of hand.

Clearly my bar pals were seeing something I couldn't see myself. But nothing was going to slow me down now that I had found a growing solution to all my "inside" problems. My company didn't see it that way and suggested I might fit in better somewhere else and fired me. It was 1952, and that experience was only the first of many painful episodes that fueled my decline into alcoholism. In spite of that, I was still at the stage where I wasn't blaming alcohol directly for any of my problems.

In my pursuit of money to both repay debts and finance my drinking, I began playing the horses, the poker machines, and the lotteries. Before I knew it, I had a serious gambling addiction. To make things even worse, I joined a men's social club that enabled me to both drink and gamble beyond normal licensed hours and certainly far beyond my means.

Then, job-wise, I made another serious mistake. I accepted a two-year contract to work for the Australian government in Port Moresby, Papua New Guinea, which was almost a frontier town in those days. I took the job because the pay was so good and I desperately needed the money to feed both of my addictions.

I didn't know what I was getting myself into, since there was little else to do in the tropics but drink and gamble. It was simply the way of life there. I had the grandiose title of commerce officer for the Papua New Guinea Copra Marketing Board. Copra is the dried kernel of the coconut, an important ingredient in manufacturing soaps and cosmetics. The British-based Bank Line of cargo ships called on schedule to plantations on the mass of islands in that part of the tropics to load their copra.

My daily job was to radio-advise plantation owners of such schedules—exacting work that suited my perfectionist-among-perfectionists nature. I was housed in the single men's quarters some six miles out of Moresby. I couldn't drink during the day because of my job, but made up for it by getting plastered almost every night, usually alone.

Upon completion of my contract, I returned home to Sydney with the standard three months' pay that went with such contracts. But everything I'd earned over the previous two years I had drunk or gambled away. At this point I knew I had a major drinking problem, but I didn't know how to get out from under it. I moved back in with my parents and managed to better control my drinking and secure a trainee position with a major Sydney department store. Although it was a struggle, I held that job for two years until it came to an inevitable end.

I awoke one Sunday morning in January 1956, recovering from the previous night's bender. I had a pounding headache and felt terrible. I turned on the radio to get the weather. Instead, I found myself caught up in a radio talk show by the then-retired Reverend Sturge Harty about the "fledgling fellowship" known as Alcoholics Anonymous and how it was helping problem drinkers. As I sat there shaking and sweating, I felt as though he was talking directly to me. When he finished, I decided to look into this fellowship to see how it might at least slow down my drinking. Then I shook my head and thought, "What a laugh."

In his talk, Sturge Harty said there was a regular Sunday night meeting up at Kings Cross, which was adjacent to downtown Sydney. Though I didn't think it could help, I decided to go anyway.

At that time, there were three inner-city and about fifteen suburban AA meetings in Sydney, twelve years after the actual arrival of Alcoholics Anonymous in Australia. I was just turning twenty-seven when I walked into the "Cross" meeting the following Sunday. As I said, although part of me was still very much in denial—"C'mon now, you're too young to be an alcoholic"—the inner me, kept hidden with great care, knew that I indeed had a real drinking problem.

While I qualified for membership from that very first meeting, I wasn't quite ready to admit I was really whipped. It took me another two-and-a-half years of slipping and sliding and a complete breakdown in my health before I finally hit my rock bottom.

During this period of on-and-off attendance at AA meetings (mostly off), I landed an executive position with a company known as the Carpenter Group operating throughout the South Pacific islands. They owned emporiums, trading vessels, and sole-agencies throughout the Fiji Islands, Tonga, Samoa, Cook Islands, Tahiti, Papua New Guinea, and the Solomons. I worked out of their Sydney head office, mostly in the retail side of the business. Much of my work had to do with interviewing potential suppliers, which inevitably included entertaining them. Somehow I was able to control my drinking so that management didn't know just how serious my problem was.

I finally hit bottom on June 25, 1958. I had arrived at my parents' home in Sydney from a business trip to Melbourne, totally exhausted from a sustained week of supplier interviews and heavy drinking. I virtually collapsed into my bed and began vomiting. This continued overnight and became violent retching the following day until the doctor was called. He diagnosed me with a severe case of hepatitis that took me nine weeks to recover from sufficiently enough to return to work.

Fortunately, I continued to receive a salary during this

time, so I was able to regain my health without the additional anxiety of lost income. But more important, during that period, I began to reflect on those last thirty months and realized they were not a complete waste. I had come to see it was God's way of bringing this stubborn alcoholic to his knees so that I could finally hit bottom and begin walking toward recovery. At last I understood what we mean in AA when we say, "No pain, no gain."

During that recovery period, I also reflected on the quality sharing I had heard at AA over the previous two and a half years. I read and digested lots of AA literature, especially the Big Book, which I read cover to cover. And, as with cream rising to the surface, I was more fully able to understand what is meant by "Just for today" (living in the now), "Let go, let God" (living with my limitations), and "First things first." Once back at meetings, I started to listen, really listen, without being quite so inhibited by the character defect of "selective hearing" I'd been suffering from. Yes, finally I was beginning to listen and identify with what I heard.

I was only back at work in Sydney about a month when I was informed that I was being transferred to our Suva office in Fiji. Since my doctor felt my health had improved enough to accept the transfer, I agreed to go. But I had one private caveat—that I must have access to AA.

One old-timer at my Kings Cross group suggested that I register myself as a "loner" with AA's General Service Office in New York (GSONY). He said they had a special program to keep in touch with "loners" all over the world. I followed his advice, but my Higher Power wanted to be sure I would have more support.

Soon after arriving in Suva, I met Ralph W. through the Suva-based doctor who was now treating my hepatitis. Our meeting was one of those "coincidences" that are really quiet miracles where God chooses to remain anonymous. Within a month, we got the first AA meeting started on the island.

While it grew slowly at first, over the next three years it developed into a mini–United Nations, with Aussies, Kiwis (New Zealanders), Poms (Englishmen), an on-and-off Fijian (Josepha), and an Indian (Ram Sami). Numbers would increase significantly when a cruise ship out of San Francisco or Long Beach, California, would stop over in Suva. We'd signal the purser before their arrival that "any friends of Bill W. on board would be most welcome at noon that day to meet with like friends at the Bailey Clinic next to the Overseas Terminal." We met wonderful AA friends that way.

Then God presented me with one of the greatest gifts in my life—my wife, Peggy. As a highly qualified and experienced nurse, she had arrived in Fiji from her home in New Zealand only a week before me to become the new matron of Lautoka Hospital. She was the perfect partner for me for three important reasons. First, she was and is the most loving and caring person one could ever meet. Second, she was a nondrinker. And third, with her wide experience and understanding of the effects of illnesses like hepatitis, Peggy became a great help in my complete recovery.

Since, as I said before, drinking is a way of life in the tropics, I thanked God many times over for my hepatitis. While that may sound strange, it was a great "insurance policy" in my early sobriety, a constant warning about what just one drink could do to me.

Peggy and I got married in October 1959, a year after we met. Today we have three splendid sons and a wonderful, loving daughter. To date, they have blessed us with ten terrific grandchildren. They all like to tease us about their having so many "honorary" aunts and uncles, these being the large number of AAs I've been privileged to sponsor over the years, many of whom are like family to our kids. My Higher Power has been so generous to me that it's difficult to describe how grateful I am.

Peggy and I have always worked to make sure our kids

grew up with strong and enduring values, the kind I was able to bring into my marriage from the AA program. Thus, I am pleased to report that not one of them has turned out to be a "loner" or a fearful and scarred alcoholic like I was growing up. And when it comes to practicing our faith, I've often told my family that "I go to church to worship God but I go to AA to serve him." They understand.

Let me share one more great family blessing with you. In June 2008, I celebrated fifty years of sobriety. A little more than a year later, in October 2009, Peggy and I celebrated fifty years of marriage—our golden wedding anniversary. That wouldn't have happened without AA.

Shortly after we left Fiji in late 1961, I changed careers. Despite my Aussie roots, my wife talked me into settling in New Zealand, something I've never regretted. We settled in Auckland, where I found a job in the trade magazine publishing field. I never thought I'd remain in print media until the day I retired some forty years later. When the New Zealand edition of *Time* magazine was launched in 1966, I was taken on as ad sales manager and eight months later made overall manager. Although this job required heavy entertaining obligations, by keeping close to my AA program and AA friends, it was never a burden.

Twenty years later, I was hired by the New Jersey–based *Journal of Commerce (JOC)*, where I worked until my retirement in 2002. The positions I held with these two publishing houses led to numerous business trips to the States, particularly their Manhattan business offices. This allowed me to visit AA's General Service Office regularly and meet with the splendid "trusted servants" who managed GSONY.

On one of my earliest visits, November 1969, I had the good fortune to secure a twenty-minute meeting with our cofounder Bill W. This was an experience I will never forget. When Bill learned I was from New Zealand, he immediately inquired about my sponsor, Ian McE. Ian had contacted Bill following his last detoxification at a New Zealand psychiatric hospital. At the hospital, Ian had picked up a copy of the *Reader's Digest* that reprinted Jack Alexander's 1941 article from the *Saturday Evening Post* entitled, "The Fledgling Organization—Alcoholics Anonymous."

Ian immediately wrote to the address given in the article asking for more information. When that letter arrived on Bill W.'s desk, he got his secretary, Bobby, to immediately ship off three copies of the Big Book. Upon receipt, Ian never drank again. That was 1946 and marked the arrival of AA in New Zealand.

Right off Ian helped start AA meetings throughout New Zealand. He kept in regular touch with Bill back in New York, culminating with a face-to-face meeting in mid-1969 when Ian visited Bill at GSONY, appropriately enough as our first world service representative.

Sharing all of this reminds me again of that brief visit I had with Bill W. in 1969, just two years before he passed away. As he bade me farewell, he made this searching comment, "Well, Don, it's still the same, isn't it—the battle with the ego, the battle with self."

As I left Bill's office that day and headed across town to my hotel, I reflected on the gentle warning he had given me. I thought, "Keep your feet on the ground, fella," as I was in the midst of attending an important publishing conference at the Time-Life Building. Wasn't I something! Ergo the ego trap . . . and "the battle with self." Then I stopped and smiled, realizing there needn't be a battle anymore, once we've given ourselves totally to this wonderful program of ours and "handed our will and our lives over to the care of God as we understood Him."

In concluding my story, I would like to share the four basic things that have helped me maintain my sobriety over the years:

1. Attend meetings—that means regularly. Only at an AA meeting will I hear what a dear friend from the Deep South describes as "what ails me." Or, as one of our old-timers here says, "to get my medicine." *Only* at an AA meeting will I hear the truth about my disease with the bonus of perhaps being of help to others.

2. Work the Steps—not just *doing* Steps but *working* them in my life. I might appear to have it all together in AA, but what am I like at home? Or at work? I've found that the degree of peace I enjoy in my heart and mind is in direct proportion to how I'm working the program in my life.

3. Trust God—which is far more than simply recognizing his existence. My soul sickness began to leave me the day I started to place my trust in my Higher Power. For me, it's been an ongoing process, but one thing I know: when I practice unconditional trust in God, all is well in my life.

4. Help others—by carrying the message. There's nothing more rewarding, and there are limitless opportunities: simply sharing at meetings, Twelfth Stepping, sponsoring, or just being a trusted servant of the fellowship. By simply shifting my attention to helping someone else, I've got my mind off *me*, and as Bill W. says in our literature: "Of all the obsessions, the greatest obsession of all for the alcoholic is the obsession with self."

Not exactly Einstein stuff, is it? But it's certainly the stuff of successful sobriety for this profoundly grateful member of Alcoholics Anonymous.

*"A seed was planted, and eleven years
later it bloomed into a sober life."*

THE STORY OF FRANK C.

'll never forget that wintry day in December 1946 when I
was first approached about going to the program of Alcoholics Anonymous. I had just returned home to Cleveland
from a short stint in Japan with the United States Army. This
particular afternoon was spent drinking in one of the local
west side saloons. When I was about to get in my car to leave,
a couple of AA guys, Darby W. and Jack B., approached the
car. They said, "Hey Frank, why don't you come with us down
to the AA club? We've got some guys your age down there and
they would love to see ya." They told me that the clubhouse
was at Sixty-fifth Street and Detroit. It was formerly the Irish
American Club (which I had been thrown out of before).

Well, I was much too busy to hear any of this. Besides, I
was just about to be discharged from the service and was
planning to go back to my job at the local brewery.

I was born in June 1927, the youngest of ten children. My dad was a barber who never drank at all. He had taken a pledge many years before through the Catholic Church and never picked up a drink. Of course, I took many pledges through the years, but I drank enough for the both of us and a few more.

My drinking started at a very young age, probably around thirteen, and progressed from there. Once I started drinking, I was a big shot. I had older brothers who were drafted, which made me and others like me more popular. All of a sudden we were the oldest. It was like we became big shots overnight. I was already beginning to get into trouble, and my parents were concerned.

After the eighth grade, my sister Lou (Lucille) and I went to Minnesota for a visit with relatives. One day during the visit, Lou told to me she was returning home to Cleveland but I would be staying in Minnesota to attend high school. That didn't make me too happy, but I went along with it. My grades were average or a little below, and I certainly knew how to get into trouble. My parents probably sent me there thinking that I'd get in less trouble if I was away from my buddies in Cleveland.

Of course, the following summer I returned home and picked up right where I had left off—down at the train yards hanging out and partying. Since I had older brothers, every-one knew me, and I was liked by almost everyone.

Looking back, it's kind of funny how I got started work-ing for the Erin Brewery. It was the summer of 1944 and I was working part-time at the railroad yard, sweeping off the passenger train cars for eighty-three cents an hour. Some of us younger guys did that for extra money during the summer breaks from school. The cars mostly carried military men at the time. That morning a neighbor named Johnny suggested that I become his helper at the brewery. He said, "You'll get eighty-one cents an hour and all the free beer that you want to drink."

Well, that was it—I had arrived! I immediately quit high school and went to work with him. This was what I wanted. I could make money and drink. It was never social drinking for me. I drank because I liked what it did for me.

My drinking continued through my teens. When I was seventeen most of the young drivers at the brewery were being called up to serve in the war, so I filled in for them. That didn't last long, though, because once I turned eighteen, I was drafted and sent overseas.

While in the army in Japan I worked at a warehouse that handled food for the military. My alcoholism progressed while I was over there. Because it was the end of the war, I only had to stay in the service for eighteen months. I could have stayed longer, but the brewery sounded better to me.

I got back from Japan, moved in with my mother, and returned to work at the brewery. I would drink and work, and work and drink. After work, I would go home for dinner and then walk up to the tavern. By the time I was twenty years old I was drinking all the time, getting into scrapes, and occasionally being picked up by the police. Being one of ten kids helped me, though, because my brother Bernie became a cop. Whenever I got into a jam, he would bail me out. The cops would grab me but would take me home or let me go when they found out I was Bernie's brother.

Even though I was invited to attend AA back in December of 1946, I didn't attend a meeting until sometime in 1947. Alcoholics Anonymous was something I had heard about years before, when I used to hang out at the train yard. We would see some guys down there who would talk with us, and when they saw us drinking, they would say they were saving us a spot at AA. Of course, we would just laugh and carry on. They were great guys, though, and always nice to us.

I continued to drink after my first meeting, but I kept going to meetings, too. AA guys like Twitter G. and Buena M. would call on me and take me on trips with them from Cleveland to Akron. We would stop at St. Thomas Hospital and go to meetings there. That was where I met Dr. Bob Smith. What a great guy! I remember he would smile at me and say, "I see they dragged you down here again, kid." It seemed like he was always pouring the coffee.

I never became friends with Doc, but I did get to see him at meetings through the late forties whenever I went to Akron. Sometimes the guys were taking a drunk with them and would stop by and grab me, too. Once they jammed me in the backseat with a spare tire and a shaking drunk, and off we went to St. Thomas in Akron.

From 1947 up until my last drink on January 20, 1957, I was what used to be called a "retread" in AA. That was because I was always in and out of the rooms of AA trying to get sober, but never quite able to put any time together. AA was big in Cleveland and there were lots of meetings. The guys were always good to me and encouraged me to keep coming. You could tell that they really wanted to see me get and stay sober.

On July 4, 1951, I married an Italian girl named Anne; we celebrated our fifty-eighth anniversary this past July. We adopted two wonderful girls and have enjoyed a full life. I like to joke and say that I gave Anne all these wonderful years. The truth is that they weren't all wonderful, but she stuck by me. For a while we had to keep moving into different apartments because we couldn't afford the thirty-eight dollars for monthly rent. My drinking was so out of hand that at times we had to rely on relatives to house us and take care of us.

Alcoholism really had a hold of me. I often say, "I'd take a drink and then the drink would take me," which was really the case with my drinking. Back then the odds of an Irishman drinking himself out of a job at the Irish brewery was about zero, but I managed to do even that. Things continued to get worse with time, but at last I finally recognized that I had a problem and needed to quit.

After some bouncing around, I eventually found a job with the Dan Dee Pretzel and Chip Company, where I worked for the next twenty-nine years. Finally, I had to retire due to back problems, among other things.

In the early fifties while I was trying to get sober, I met many wonderful people. In May 1956, I went through the program at Rosary Hall with Sister Ignatia. She was a tough one but she loved her work. When I completed the program, Sister Ignatia gave me a little book that I still read today. It was entitled *Confidence in God* and gives words of encouragement. I've worn out my copy of this wonderful book over the years. Sister Ignatia also handed out Sacred Heart medallions and told the recipients that if they were going to take a drink, they had to return the medallion first. When I asked, "Where's my medallion?" she replied, "You? No, Frank, you won't make it a week." Then she said, "I don't waste them on guys like you." She could tell I wasn't sincere.

Of course, she was right. I only made four days that time. Since I had completed the program at Rosary Hall, I could never go through it again. However, they held meetings there that people from the outside could attend. One night at a meeting Sister Ignatia introduced the speaker to me. It was Bill Wilson from New York. I stayed and listened to him talk that night, but as he finished, I excused myself to go to the restroom. Later, I was told that he had inquired where I went. One of the guys had told him that I had taken a "Duffy" on him and was probably across town drunk.

A few months later, following a long day of drinking, I drove my car off a pier into Lake Erie. Today, I jokingly tell people that I was the only member of the Edgewater Yacht Club who didn't have a boat. It happened to be the Fourth of July, which was also my fifth wedding anniversary. I was able to get out of that one with no real repercussions other than personal embarrassment. The authorities asked my wife if she thought this was an attempt at suicide. She knew it wasn't. I had only been trying to find a place to pull over for a nap.

There were so many things toward the end of my drinking that prepared me for AA. Of course, the guys in the program had really stuck with me and never gave up. My brother Billy called the AA Central Office once again. The office turned my name over to the Gordon Square Group. Although it wasn't the first time they came to get me, this time they sent Joe S. and Eddie R., who took me to the twenty-four-hour group. Over the next year, Joe and I became very close and took turns getting drunk. If he got drunk on Tuesday, I'd be drunk on Friday. Eddie, a former pro football player with a few years of sobriety under his belt, stuck in there with us during this time. He kept us going to meetings and otherwise tried to help.

On what turned out to be my last drunk, I called Joe's house. His wife, Dorothy, answered and said, "Don't call here no more. He was bad enough before he met you." So I called Eddie, and he said that he'd meet me at my brother's house. I told him I was too sick to make it over there. He said, "Well, then you don't want help." I made it to my brother's house and met Eddie. That was my last time. It was January 1957; Joe had his last drink on the nineteenth and I had mine on the twentieth. Neither of us found a reason or an excuse to take a drink since. Joe died sober, which I always say is the only graduation we ever have from AA. Eddie was the man who gave Joe and me the foundation for sobriety, and I've always been grateful to both of those men.

Again, Alcoholics Anonymous was really big in Cleveland; Clarence S. was the founder. Not just the founder of a group, but one of the founders of Alcoholics Anonymous. Before AA started Clarence would take the guys from Cleveland to Akron for meetings of the Oxford Group. However, many of these early Cleveland converts were Catholic, and the Oxford

Group was considered by the church to be a religion. The Catholic priests had told the guys that they couldn't be part of the Oxford Group or any other religion.

That caused Clarence to pull away from the Oxford Group and start a meeting here in Cleveland that became one of the earliest AA meetings.

The second group in Cleveland was called the Doan Men's Group. That group will celebrate their seventieth anniversary this year. There's a lot of AA history here in Cleveland!

It's significant to mention that just a few months after the Cleveland group broke away from the Akron Oxford Group, a series of articles about Alcoholics Anonymous was published in our local newspaper, the *Plain Dealer*. Those articles resulted in more than five hundred new AA members and thirty new groups in a very short time. If Clarence and the others hadn't started their own meetings here in Cleveland, this growth might never have occurred.

The early Cleveland members used many of the concepts from the Oxford Group, and we still follow the same traditions in the Cleveland area today. The Four Absolutes of Love, Honesty, Purity, and Unselfishness are an example. It was also a practice to "sponsor" the newcomers into AA. The groups provided instruction and classes to take the new guy through the Steps. We used the Big Book of *Alcoholics Anonymous*, *The Little Red Book*, and (one of my personal favorites) *Stools and Bottles*. We all came off those bar stools! Most of us read and gave away copies of Emmet Fox's *Sermon on the Mount*.

Another Oxford Group tradition that many of us still follow today is to pause at the podium for a prayer before starting our "lead." Usually it is the Serenity Prayer, and afterward we allow comments. The Serenity Prayer didn't come from the Oxford Group, but the practice of saying a prayer before giving a lead certainly came directly from those early guys. Another custom with the early groups was to close the meeting with the Lord's Prayer.

Throughout my sobriety I have relied heavily on the Big Book and working with others. I'm still active in the program today, but it has been somewhat limited by recent surgery related to my diabetes. Not long ago I was talking with my only surviving sibling, my sister Lou, and I asked her why I was the only one in the family with diabetes. She said, "Frank, did you ever stop to think that nobody else lived as long as you?"

I know that everything good in my life is the result of my sobriety through AA. The saying "You can't keep it unless you give it away" is one of the things that I've patterned my life after. Back in the early days, when I was newly sober, I'd take a new AA recruit with me on my potato chip route. Most of them didn't have jobs when they came in, so we could talk about AA all day long and go to meetings at night. It worked out well because I was able to stay sober by giving away what was given to me. And the guys didn't eat *too* many potato chips!

Even today I make it a priority to attend meetings. I go three or four times a week, sometimes more. The fellowship that we enjoy in AA is wonderful! I've been so fortunate to have had so many friends in my life. Over the years I've had several sponsors and feel that these relationships have been critical for my sobriety. There are several people that I'm close to now and use as sponsors. My friend Mike, who lives in Las Vegas, calls me on a regular basis. We are very close. Only in AA could I have found people such as these.

Years ago we would occasionally travel to California to visit my brother Hubert and his wife. On our first trip there I arranged to go to an AA meeting. At the meeting I introduced myself (first and last name) and told the group that I was visiting from Cleveland. After returning to my brother's home, the phone rang and the voice on the other end asked to speak to me. My sister-in-law thought it was a bit odd since I didn't know anyone in California. The man said his name was Dr. Paul O. He was in the program and wanted to get together with me. I knew the name because he had relatives in my area who owned some drugstores. Paul knew my brother because they had done business together through the years. My brother didn't know that Paul was an alcoholic. Actually, my brother and his wife knew very little about AA and alcoholism and didn't want "those AA people" coming over to their house.

I asked Paul where we should meet and he laughed and said he was on his way over. He said, "Your brother is going to fall over when he finds out that I'm in the program." He was right; my brother was shocked, which Paul and I both thought was quite funny. He was wonderful man who treated me really well. His story is in both the third and fourth editions of the Big Book.

One night we drove down to Laguna for a meeting, where Paul introduced me to Chuck C. All through Ohio and everywhere I've gone, I have found friends in the fellowship. I could go on and on relating many more such experiences, but I know it's not necessary. Only in AA could I have had this life.

This program is very simple. Its single purpose is to give the message to the next suffering alcoholic. We have an answer to the "drink problem," not to *all* problems. I sincerely hope that we keep this program simple and stick with the Traditions.

Seems to me that the best way to help the new members learn what AA is and what it isn't is to share the Twelve Traditions. The Traditions explain about our membership very well. If groups focus more on the Traditions, I believe they will have fewer problems.

My life today is full, and I really must live one day at a time. Many people have done so much for me, and I'm very grateful to all of them.

Although it took almost eleven years for the seed of sobriety to take root, it may have been exactly what I needed to be prepared for this life. If you are struggling with alcoholism, my message to you is simple: Keep going to meetings!

"Just Another Bozo on the Bus"

THE STORY OF JOHN H.

He looked across the table at me with tears rolling down his cheeks. I could feel his love as he said, "My Johnny, where have I failed you?" This was a turning point in my life. It was as if somebody had reached deep within me and pulled out my heart. I knew right then and there that I was going to have to leave that town.

It was just another snowy winter day in my hometown of Scranton, Pennsylvania, and I was getting home from drinking. I was very drunk, which was typical for me at the time. My first drink had been a little over a year earlier when I was just fifteen. I had gotten drunk and sick. From that moment forward I loved drinking. It was as if I had had a spiritual experience.

To get into my parents' house, I had to go around to the back, walk up a couple of steps, and enter through the kitchen.

That particular day I was so drunk that I only made it to the back steps before passing out. That's where my dad found me. He took me into the kitchen and fixed us some tea. It's funny, but I think the Irish thought tea was a remedy for everything. That was when he looked at me and spoke those words that pierced the deepest part of my soul. For the first time I realized that I had hurt a person who loved me dearly.

My family was wonderfully well adjusted with no real problems. There is no way that I can look back on my childhood and say that I came from a dysfunctional situation. We were just like most of the other Irish Catholic families living in that rural Pennsylvania coal-mining town.

I was born in November 1934 with eczema covering my body. I was a very sickly child. Those were difficult times for families near the end of the Great Depression. My parents had the added stress of another child and one who was sick. Medications were quite expensive, and my parents were already struggling to care for my brothers and pay the regular household bills.

When I was five, my younger brother was born. It seemed like my mother just put me down and picked him up. I felt a lot of resentment toward my younger brother, which I hung on to for a long time.

About that time my dad took me under his wing. Dad was very mechanically inclined, and I took after him. I worked with him on odd jobs and projects, getting the wrenches and stuff like that. I really admired him because he was such a caring person. For example, if the widow next door had a broken basement window, he wouldn't discuss it; he just fixed it. That was the type of role model he was for me. Everyone who knew him liked him, and he really loved and adored my mother.

I, on the other hand, didn't adore my mother because she was very domineering and things *had* to be *her* way. I remember when I was sixteen and my mother sat me down for a conversation. She had been disappointed in me since the very first time I had gotten drunk. She explained that I was by far the brightest of the boys in our family. "But you are not going to go to college," she said. "It would be a waste of time because you won't conform." My mother was right, but I held a different opinion at the time. It's a good thing she wasn't able to respond to my unspoken opinion.

I knew I needed to get away, so I joined the marines right after high school graduation. By that time my thinking had become defective, and I didn't consider that our country was in the middle of the Korean conflict. Because I was still only seventeen, I needed a parent to sign for me. My mother was glad to sign; she was more than happy to see me go.

I went to boot camp in Paris Island, South Carolina, for thirteen weeks. After completion, I was stationed at Camp Pendleton, just north of San Diego, for advanced training. It was the first time I had seen the Pacific Ocean, and I fell in love with it. I immediately knew I wanted to settle there after the service.

Eventually a group of us flew to Japan and then Korea, where I served with two different outfits. I celebrated my eighteenth birthday there, and to be honest I celebrated something almost every day. I never needed a reason to drink; it just seemed like the thing to do.

Most of my time in the marines, I was just an average grunt doing whatever was in front of me while drinking more than my share at night. I always took full advantage of the weekend passes. I'm sure you can imagine a nineteen-year-old alcoholic marine in Japan with his pockets full of money. The miracle is that I made it back to the States without being arrested.

My best job while over there was being the driver for a major. On Friday afternoons, we would leave the base. I was driving and the major was in the backseat. On Sunday evening when we returned, the major was driving and I was passed out in the backseat. Why he put up with me I'll never know, but they really didn't make a big deal out of my drinking.

A short time later, I was on my way back to California, where I planned to live after being discharged. The trip took thirty-three days, which would seem to be ample time to make plans. The problem was that I was an alcoholic and was thus making plans with defective equipment. I had convinced myself that I was going to live in Southern California and make my fortune. But first I thought what I needed to do was to get married.

So as soon as I got to California, I set out looking for some poor soul who would marry and take care of me. Even though I was a drunk, I looked hard enough that I found a taker. As it turned out, I took that young woman to places she had never planned to go. We were married just before my discharge from the marines.

During that phase of my life, my drinking had reached new levels. I began turning from Dr. Jekyll to Mr. Hyde while drinking and became violent and crazy.

I would often drink just to fall asleep. Many servicemen and women return from military tours with psychological problems and challenges. I'm sure my depression and sleeplessness were related to my time overseas and my uncontrolled alcoholism. The heavy drinking did not fix the problems but it certainly allowed me to forget them, at least for brief moments.

We moved in with my wife's mother in LA while I was looking for a job. I was drinking both night and day but knew that I had to find something. I was finally hired by the *Los Angeles Times* for a wonderful position with the potential to lead to a promising career. I was just a young marine, but I had the good fortune of working with the son of the newspaper's owner.

Within a year we already had our first child. One day I was in a horrendous automobile accident with the company car. It was a real problem, because the accident occurred in San Diego and my territory was in LA. I wasn't supposed to travel outside of my territory, and to make matters worse there was a young lady in the car who wasn't my wife. I knew I should have been fired but the only response was to take away my privilege to drive company cars. In order to keep my job, I had to buy my own car.

That incident didn't slow me down a bit. I would frequent bars during the day with my briefcase in hand, trying to convince myself I was a rising star in the newspaper business. That pattern continued, and I eventually became the only employee who was required to physically report to my boss every afternoon before leaving work for the day.

Most of the time I spent in the office was in the early morning while I was nursing my hangover from the previous night. The young copy boys caught on, and I became the brunt of their practical jokes. They loved to take the telephone off my desk, glue the receiver down, and hide the phone in my desk. They would then have somebody call me from another room and stand there laughing at me while I fumbled around trying to deal with the embarrassment.

My wife and I had two children, but our marriage was a disaster. I can remember that the kids would hide behind the sofa when I came home from work. They never knew what I would be like when I walked through the door. My wife had to listen to me falsely accuse her of turning the kids against me, like it was her fault.

Two years before I made it to Alcoholics Anonymous my family called a meeting one Saturday morning to discuss my drinking. My mother-in-law and her boyfriend did the preaching. They told me that if I continued to drink, I was going to lose everything in my life: the house, my wife, my children, my job, and my health. My response to this meeting was, "I'm going to live my life any way I want, and you people can mind your own damn business."

Within two years every single thing we had talked about had happened. My boss called me in one day and said, "John,

I'm sorry but we have to fire you, and we've told security that we don't want you back on this property." There I was, sick with a hangover and fired from my job. I drove home to our little Skid Row house owned by my mother-in-law to see a moving van in the driveway packed with all of our possessions. My wife stood there with our two young children, who looked terrified. She said, "We're moving in with my mother. Good-bye."

My first thought was, "Good, now I'll be able to drink the way I want to." I decided I could just stay at the house and sleep on the carpet because I didn't need a bed anyway. That plan was foiled because as soon as they left, the house was boarded up by a couple of men, presumably from the bank. When I protested, they told me I hadn't been paying for it so I couldn't live in it.

At that point most people would probably have called and asked to stay with a friend, but that was not an option for me. I didn't have any friends left, so I moved on. I began drinking with abandon since there was nothing else left in my life. I figured I could be comfortable in my Renault Dauphine if I could find a place to park it. After driving around for a while, I found a small lot next to an orange grove and decided to make it my home. There was plenty of room in the car for me and my two close friends, Ernest and Julio Gallo.

I don't know exactly how long I lived in the car. When I came to and saw the sun, I wouldn't know if it was coming up or going down. If I awoke and it was dark, I knew it must be nighttime.

On the morning of April 9, 1959, I opened the car door and fell onto the ground. I kneeled there throwing up blood, which wasn't a new thing for me. But on that particular day I had a feeling unlike anything before, a feeling that I could sink no lower. It was complete despair. At that moment I uttered the words, "Please, God, help me! Please, God, help me!"

Immediately I had the thought, "Call Alcoholics Anonymous." I had never heard of AA, and didn't know anything about the organization. I just heard this message and knew I had better call.

After cleaning up a bit, I drove back to LA and stopped at a drugstore to use a pay phone. I called information but rather than giving me the number the operator said, "Just a moment." She put me through directly to Alcoholics Anonymous. A lady named Sybil answered. She told me where the Southwest Alano AA Club was and asked if I would be able to get there. I told her I could.

When I arrived at the address I was surprised to see that the club was right in the middle of my old newspaper territory. I had been by there hundreds of times and never noticed it. When I approached the door, it opened from the inside. A little old man looked at me as he extended his hand and said, "My name is Joe; what's yours?"

I guess I told him my name, although I really don't remember my response. Joe later told me I had asked him two questions: "How do I become a member? How much are the dues?"

He replied, "Kiddo, if you step across the threshold, you can become a member. As far as the dues are concerned, it's apparent that you've already paid yours."

That was my introduction to AA. I stayed for the meeting and some fellowship afterward, but I don't recall much of that afternoon. I do remember being given all the pamphlets they had at that time, which wasn't too many. I drove back out to the orange grove and parked under a light. That evening I read. I was even given a pamphlet entitled "To the Woman Alcoholic." I guess they figured it wouldn't hurt.

The next morning I headed right back to the Alano Club since they had told me to come back. Once again I was greeted by Joe, who told me that he was going to be my temporary sponsor. He drove an old Chevy and he had a system. The newcomer had to sit on the hump in the backseat. As the month progressed and more newcomers came aboard, you could move to a better seat. Eventually you were sitting right up front next to Joe; then you were out.

The meetings I attended in LA at that time always had a row of seats against the wall for newcomers. They called it "Newcomers' Row." During the meeting they asked if there were any newcomers. That was it. They didn't want to know your name and they didn't want to hear another word from you. Sometimes I think that was a pretty good idea.

After thirty days, Joe introduced me to a guy named Howard. He said, "Everyone calls him Howdy, and he's your new sponsor." Howdy and I chatted a bit, and he asked me where I lived. Well, I didn't want to tell him that after thirty days of sobriety I was still living in my car. But I had no choice.

He said, "Okay, you're going to come home with me and stay in my basement." I couldn't believe that this guy who had just met me was going to take me into his home and make me welcome. Over the next few weeks I did some household chores and cleaned the pool to earn my room and board.

Howdy was my first real sponsor. We had a great relationship. He took me through the first three Steps of the program. After a while he said, "John, I want you to go down to the *LA Times* newspaper and make amends." Going back and facing them was not high on my priority list, but I was staying at his house and eating his food, so with a sense of obligation I followed his directions.

I met with my old boss and explained the course I was on now with AA. He looked at me and said, "John, how would you like your old job back?" I nearly fell over. I wasn't expecting my job back at all; I was just doing what AA had taught me. Before I could get too excited, he said, "By the way, the territory was so messed up by the time you left, no one has been able to make a living with it since."

It is absolutely amazing what happened to me once I was working and sober. I showed up, did my job, and got results.

I went to meetings at night and things just continued to get better. One day Howdy told me the time had come for me to move out. I found another member of AA to share a garage apartment with me. I could write an entire book about the year John K. and I lived together. We remain very close friends to this day, both of us with more than fifty years of sobriety.

Just before my one-year AA birthday, I decided it was time to get rid of the Renault Dauphine that still smelled like wine. I found a dealer willing to take the car on a trade-in and bought a 1957 Triumph TR3. I thought I had died and gone to heaven. I took the top off so I could enjoy the Southern California sunshine and never put it back on.

Shortly after, I was driving down one of the newer freeways not really thinking about anything in particular. I suddenly realized the driver to my right and the one to my left were both staring at me. I couldn't imagine what they were looking at. Then it dawned on me that I was singing as loudly as I could to the song on the radio. That was when I knew the joy of sobriety and was truly grateful for being sober.

All of this happened before I was one year sober. It was many years before I recognized that God, in his infinite grace, had removed my obsession to drink shortly after I came to Alcoholics Anonymous. The obsession has never returned. At the time I thought it was the meetings, or my sponsor, or possibly the fellowship. I never gave God credit until much later in my sobriety. It has become much easier to see in hindsight than it was when I was experiencing it in my daily life.

After five years back with the newspaper, it was time for me to move on. The paper had made some major ownership changes. Even though I was doing very well with them, I knew that I needed to leave.

A friend who had become my business mentor helped me get my next job, which turned out to be a dream job. The company was headquartered in Wisconsin, but I was being hired as the regional sales manager for the western United States and Hawaii. The company insisted I fly first class when traveling and stay in a suite at the better hotels. I had a lucrative expense account and wasn't allowed to pay for anything with my own money. All along I took care of my responsibilities, such as child support payments.

It was great! I could travel and work and since I was single, I went to AA meetings everywhere I went. The job went along very well, and after about two years, the directors from Wisconsin called and asked to meet with me in Palm Springs. We had dinner; then they told me that the company's vice president of sales had been let go, and they offered me the position. They explained that it would require a move to Wisconsin. Initially, I was reluctant, but they kept raising the stakes until I just couldn't refuse.

Although I was seven years sober at this point, my story illustrates that sanity does not necessarily follow sobriety. I had been dating a girl who was *almost* sober. She also had a couple of kids. My defective thinking told me it would be a good idea to get married and move my ready-made family to Wisconsin. Please note that even though I had seven years without a drink, I had only thoroughly completed the first three Steps of the AA program.

The drive for money, property, and prestige was on. I stayed very busy with my work and excelled as the VP. My family life was horrible, and I was only a visitor to AA. I think it's important to mention that I was traveling extensively and attended meetings on the road. I had no home group and no real sponsor. Today I am 100 percent certain it is only through God's grace that I remained sober during that period of time. I have learned that complacency causes many alcoholics to get off track and leads some back to drinking.

Things continued that way for five years until I decided to try a geographical cure for my problems. I moved my family to Atlanta and started a new business with a partner named

Sam. We worked really hard at developing the business, and it became quite successful. My marriage and home life were failing miserably.

After seven years in Atlanta, my wife and I were through. Although we had been married for twelve years, it was one of those marriages that should have never happened.

About that time I traveled to New York to visit one of our showrooms and decided to attend an AA meeting. I went to Midtown, which had two meetings. The first one was for the street people and the later one was for the "elites," which is what I considered myself to be.

I arrived early and went inside to the "street people meeting" wearing the finest clothes money can buy. The thought came to me that I needed to hang up my coat. Just as that thought entered my mind, I knew I couldn't—somebody would steal it. Suddenly those thoughts terrorized me. What had I become? I had been sober for nineteen years and was sicker than I had been after one year. I could see that "self-reliance" was failing me, and I had become an egotistical phony. The only thing missing from total alcoholic ruin was the alcohol.

That night I packed up, called my sponsor in LA, and headed back there. For the next thirty days, we went through the Twelve Steps of AA. I finally started cleaning up the wreckage of my life, as I should have done many years before. Howdy was a lifesaver, and I'll always have a special place in my heart for him.

During my time in LA, I also attended a weekend retreat conducted by a Catholic priest known in AA as Father John Doe. His real name was Father Ralph Pfau. It was there that I did my Fourth Step. I also shared my Fifth Step with him. That was when I first began to feel the nearness of my Creator. My life took on new meaning, and AA became more than just a place to go; it truly became a way of life.

Once I returned to Atlanta, my wife and I finalized the

divorce. My partner, Sam, called me one day and said he was running late getting to work. A few hours later I learned he had committed suicide. Thank God I had been through the Steps and was now living my life by the spiritual principles of AA.

I finally realized that the foundation of my life was a spiritual one. I no longer needed the approval of anyone because I could finally love myself. With this foundation and God's grace, I was able to build a new life with a new purpose. Being of service took on a whole new meaning for me. I became very active in AA and have remained so ever since.

My life has been blessed by a wonderful woman who has been my wife for over twenty-seven years. Her name is Mary Emma, and she is the love of my life. We have traveled all over the world together and currently live in Hilton Head. We are both active in the program and are surrounded by countless blessings.

My advice to anyone, freely given, is to work through the Twelve Steps completely. I currently sponsor several men and enjoy watching them grow in the program. I'm so proud to be invited into their lives. I also have a sponsor today who is a dear friend and a mighty good example of AA.

As I mentioned at the beginning of the story, I was born into a solid family. I am fortunate that I was able to make amends to them and be the son I couldn't be earlier. One day I asked my dad if he knew when I had first started drinking. He said, "Oh yeah, we knew exactly when you started." He went upstairs, then came back carrying a shoebox and dumped the contents onto the table. There lay all my report cards from when I was growing up. He looked at a few, stopped with one in his hand, and said, "This is when you started drinking, right here."

When I got my first Big Book the price was only $3.50, but I didn't have the money. The group financed the book, and I had to pay thirty-five cents a week until it was paid off. I believe the message was one of the most powerful ever given to me in Alcoholics Anonymous: "There are no freebies, but we're here to help." That you have, and I'm most thankful and grateful. After fifty years of sobriety, today I'm happy just being "another Bozo on the bus."

"My motto used to be, 'Take something, you'll feel better.' I felt so good sometimes that it almost killed me."

THE STORY OF JOHN K.

It was a beautiful Sunday morning in May of 1937. I was seven years old at the time and driving with my family to Saint Ann's Catholic Church in Seal Beach, California, where I was to receive my First Holy Communion—a major event in the Catholic religion.

My father was at the wheel. His handsome Irish face was beet red, which meant he had been out very late with "the boys" the night before and was still hung over. My always suspicious brain also deduced this from the blowout I heard him and my mother having when he came rolling in "legless" as usual. They would throw things at each other and tear the place apart . . . and then usually kiss and make up the next morning.

But on this particular Sunday morning she was still very angry because today was supposed to be such a special religious occasion. I was crammed in the backseat between my older brother, Jimmy, and my younger sister, Pat, but I could still see the steam coming out of my mother's ears as she kept glaring at my old man.

As the car swerved around a corner, I held on to the front seat to avoid bumping into my sister, who always complained to my mother that I was leaning on her. Lo and behold, I found a peanut wedged into the crack behind the seat. Now the good nuns at school had been telling us for months that we had to fast before receiving communion, that we couldn't have anything to eat or drink or else we'd be committing a mortal sin. But boy, was I hungry, and that peanut looked so tempting.

I glanced around to make sure nobody was watching, then shoved the peanut into my mouth, chewed it quickly, and swallowed it. Suddenly I realized I was going to hell. I had just committed a mortal sin, which are things like murder, rape, and adultery. I was only seven and I had already hit the big time. But I sure wasn't going to tell anybody. It would be my secret until the Devil came and got me. As I look back now, I think that was the day I became a pathological liar.

That incident was only one of the things that contributed to my low self-esteem as a child. Being a bed wetter was another thing that made me feel bad about myself. I was constantly teased about that by my sisters and brother and whacked across the head by my mother. But she would always apologize and tell me she was only trying to whack some sense into me. I had sense. I just couldn't hold my water.

Maybe it was that kind of stuff that made me a troublesome kid, or maybe my self-will just ran riot from the day I popped out of my mother's womb. Either way, I believe I was always an alcoholic just waiting for his first drink.

I was born an Irish Catholic and raised in Los Angeles. I remember being a fearful little kid and a crybaby. But by the time I started school, I could no longer hold those bad feelings inside, and they came out as the class clown and the guy always looking for attention. I'd do things like drop a book on the floor or tickle one of the girls when we were supposed to be reciting the Pledge of Allegiance or the Lord's Prayer. The poor nun would send me to the principal's office, where Sister Superior would glare at me until I felt I had to go to the bathroom. Then she'd whack me across the knuckles with a huge ruler, and I'd go back to class holding out my hands like they were a badge of honor.

Growing up I really liked girls, but I was short and skinny and always felt clumsy around them. When I'd try to put the make on them, they'd usually run away laughing. I did finally get a childhood sweetheart. She was always very nice to me, probably because I never tried to put the make on her. When I became a merchant seaman in my teens, we would write to each other. I found that when I was drunk it was easy to tell her how much I loved her in a letter. I could pretend she loved me that much, too.

My father was my hero. I loved to listen to him sing and whistle and tell jokes at parties. In fact, I had my first drink with my dad when I was nine. He let me have a small glass of beer, but no more. He always warned me about getting drunk and the trouble it caused. I was only fifteen when he died, and it tore me all to pieces. That's also when my drinking and drugging really took off.

My mother also had a good sense of humor, which I think helped her survive all the problems in our family. She kept her hurts deep down inside. In March 1947, when my older brother, Jimmy, and I decided to leave home to work as merchant seamen on cargo ships, she simply smiled and wished us luck. I was only sixteen and weighed about a hundred pounds. I could tell my mother felt bad about my going, but she never tried to talk me out of it.

Jimmy, who by now was a heavy drinker and heroin user, already had his card in the Seamen's Union. He helped me get my Coast Guard papers just before we left by bus for Galveston,

Texas, which was then a very large oil drilling center and shipping port.

The day after we arrived and began looking for work, tragedy struck the nearby town of Texas City. It was late afternoon when one of the large cargo ships docked there filled with ammonia nitrate—something you can make bombs from—caught fire and exploded. That set fire to two other large vessels carrying ammonia nitrate. When they both blew up, fire spread to a row of nearby oil tankers. Some of those ships were blown so far out of the water that they set fire to docks and warehouses and nearby parts of Texas City. My brother and I felt the earth tremble all the way in Galveston.

Jimmy and I volunteered to go into Texas City to help with the cleanup, mainly because they promised to feed us. We had little money left and were real hungry. When I saw all those burned and broken bodies, I got really drunk and stayed drunk all the while we were there. When we finally returned to Galveston, we discovered that a lot of cargo ships there were short on crews due to the Texas City explosions. So my brother managed to get me an emergency union card, and we shipped out on a gas tanker named *McKitrick Hills*, headed for France. I worked in the engine room as a "wiper," otherwise known as the guy who cleans up the place.

For the next six years, I got drunk and high on every ship I sailed and in every port we entered. Trouble also found me in almost every port—from Singapore to Yokohama, from Malaysia to Panama, from Cairo to Hamburg. The booze and drugs made me feel six feet ten and 300 pounds of sheer muscle, but I'd wake up in the jail a skinny, 120-pound angry drunken kid.

Although I was given the great privilege of sailing around the world several times over, sadly I remember very little of it. Most of the things I do remember have to do with drinking and drugging—like falling in love with Hildegarde, a lady of the night in Paris whose affection I lost by throwing up in her lap; like trying to learn how to smoke a hubbly, bubbly pipe in Saudi Arabia, only to have the lit hashish fall out and burn the hair off my chest; or like walking into a crowded dance hall in Japan and later waking up on the sidewalk outside after being beaten up by some guy I was drinking with.

My daily program became "take something, you'll feel better." I had no idea that at age seventeen I was headed for a real train wreck. Drinking made me feel invisible and bulletproof. I thought bad things only happened to other people—like my brother, Jimmy, who died of a heroin overdose. I was very fortunate not to have trouble with drugs like heroin, but the truth is, I just didn't like drugs all that much. I took them when they were around but I mostly drank. I drank and I drank and I drank.

By 1950 I needed a respite, so I took some time off. I had been sending some money home to my mother, and she had been saving it for me. My childhood sweetheart was still there waiting for me, and we decided to get married. She knew I drank a lot but so did her father and two brothers. She seemed okay with it—until she really saw me in action.

She got pregnant just before I shipped out again. My first daughter, Darlene, was almost seven months old before I came back. My wife asked me to book shorter trips, so I did. She soon became sorry she made this request, because every time I was home, I was bringing my drinking buddies back to our small apartment and having loud, drunken parties. By 1953, she had had enough. She packed up and left, taking our daughter with her. I was so drunk, I didn't even try to stop her. I sat in that apartment for several weeks just drinking and feeling sorry for myself. The only thing I remember is having a hard time falling asleep.

One day when I ran out of booze, I staggered into my car and headed for a liquor store. Driving through a busy intersection, I fell asleep at the wheel and drove under a large tractor trailer. The whole top of my car was sheared off, almost taking my head with it. I jokingly say my Olds 88 became an Olds 44.

But it was really no laughing matter. My left arm was pushed back behind my shoulder blade, the skin was torn off my other arm, my skull and four ribs were fractured, and three fingers were severed from my left hand. I was in the Harbor General Hospital in Long Beach, California, for more than two months. That's where I got hooked on pain pills. There was a guy in my room worse off than me who needed more pain pills than I got. Sometimes he'd be asleep when the nurse would come by. She'd leave his pain pills on his tray, and I'd manage to crawl out of bed and get them before he woke up. When he'd look for the pills, I'd tell him he had already taken them. I did feel a little bit guilty when he'd lie there moaning all night.

When I finally got out of the hospital, I was dead broke. So I shipped out once again. This time things went from bad to worse. I was now drunk all the time and developed a real bad reputation. Nobody wanted to work with me. In 1955 I finally got blackballed for drinking, and the union yanked my card. Back then, the Seamen's Union only did that to Communists and real bad drunks.

I wound up moving back in with my mother. By now she was a pretty heavy drinker herself, so it worked out for a while. When I didn't have much money, I'd go to the drugstore and buy terpin hydrate and codeine cough syrup, which contained a goodly amount of alcohol. The trouble was, I drank so much of it that I couldn't cough until I finally sobered up.

At one point I fell into a deep depression. I wasn't allowed to see my daughter. I couldn't get any work. I had the sweats and the shakes. I felt there was no point of living anymore, so I went into the bathroom one night and slashed my wrists— not too deep because you could get hurt that way. But it was enough for my mother to insist that I see a psychiatrist. I did, and he told me that once he got my thinking straightened out, I'd be able to drink normally. I think he needed to see a psychiatrist. But my suicide attempt taught me one important thing. Alcoholics don't really want to die; they just don't know how to live.

My mother finally had enough and threw me out. I was now twenty-five. No one in the family was willing to take me in, and my friends were as bad off as I was. So I started the rounds of living in cheap motels and flophouses. When all my money was finally gone, I lived in wrecked cars, in doorways, and on the street. I would either beg for money or scheme for it. Alcoholics can be pretty good schemers when the situation calls for it.

I became a dealer in used tires. Actually I would steal tires at night off parked cars and sell them rather cheaply to dealerships that would turn a blind eye. I wore an old Texaco T-shirt I had found at the Salvation Army, so that anyone who got suspicious would think I worked for Texaco. The T-shirt read: "You can trust the man with the star."

Then the time came when I knew I had to stop drinking or I would die. A fellow in a bar had told me about Alcoholics Anonymous but said it didn't work, so I never thought much about it until the fall of 1956. I got so sick that I wound up in the detox unit at Park Avenue Hospital in Los Angeles. I had the DTs and thought the orderlies who were strapping me down were trying to kill me. I saw great big insects and heard someone calling a football game. They finally double-dosed me with paraldehyde, and I passed out.

When I came out of my fog, I was on the medical ward being treated for a liver problem. I noticed the fellow in the next bed had a group of guys around him laughing and joking. I heard someone mention Alcoholics Anonymous and others talk about Steps and slogans. They were there the next day, too. My roommate's name was Kenny, a member of AA, and these were guys from his group. He was there for stomach surgery and was leaving the next day. That night he talked to me about trying the program, gave me his name and phone number, and told me to call him when I left the hospital. I said I would, but I didn't.

It wasn't until my fifth arrest for being drunk and disorderly and the judge threatening to throw the book at me if he ever saw me in his court again that I finally hit bottom and knew I couldn't go on like this. For some reason I had kept Kenny's phone number in my shabby wallet. I called him, and he took me to my first AA meeting the next day. He gave me an AA Big Book and became my first sponsor. That was March 19, 1957, Saint Joseph's Day. And I haven't found it necessary to take a drink since.

Kenny realized what bad shape I was in and knew I needed some additional support to make it. So he got me into the Alcovery Center to dry out and then into a halfway house for three months. It was at that halfway house that I finally became willing to go to any lengths to stay sober. I mopped floors, cleaned the toilets, did the laundry, and even helped cook some meals without burning the soup. Slowly it all began to build up my self-esteem.

I needed a job to pay for my share at the house. By now I had God back in my life, and he introduced me to a fellow named Roger at a meeting one night. Roger was a roofer and needed some additional guys on his crew. The very next day he took me to a pawn shop, bought me some used tools, and by the end of the week I was helping him shingle a roof. He started to teach me how to do all kinds of roofs—tar, shingle, tile. It became my profession. I was now realizing that God, who I always believed in but walked away from, was helping me put my life back together.

One day I received a frantic phone call from my mother. My brother, Jimmy, had come home in real bad shape, and she was trying to help him get well. She had gone into his room that morning to wake him up but couldn't. I raced over to the house to find Jimmy dead from a heroin overdose. The needle was still on the floor next to the bed. He was only thirty-two.

I loved my brother and cried over him like a little baby. I kept asking why was I now sober and he had to die like this. Then I began thinking that he was my big brother and was always trying to teach me something. Maybe Jimmy wanted to show me in this tragic manner what would happen to me if I kept drinking and drugging. I pray for him every single day.

Jimmy's death reinforced my determination to make Alcoholics Anonymous the most important thing in my life. I knew that without it, I wouldn't even have a life. So I became very active in AA—I made coffee, chaired meetings, cleaned up, put the Twelve Steps into my life, and became of service to the program and to my fellow drunks. As they say in the fellowship, if you don't drink, make meetings, and work the Twelve Steps, your life will get better whether you want it to or not. I wanted it to and it did.

Roger, who owned the company I worked for, had a son with a serious asthma problem. He wanted to move to a different climate, so I went to school, got my state license, and bought the business from him for a reasonable price. I couldn't believe I now owned my own business. It was another gift from my Higher Power.

I tried to get back with my first wife, my childhood sweetheart, but she was very ill and died of emphysema. Our daughter, Darlene, started drinking and drugging. Thank God, today she's in the AA program and we're very close.

I moved from Los Angeles to Chino Hills, where my business grew even more. I met a lovely woman in my AA group there, and we got married. She had two sons I helped raise, and we had a daughter together, Diana, the love of my life.

God has given me the privilege of sponsoring many guys since I got sober. I take them to meetings in my old Caddy, which they nicknamed "The Wet Brain Express" after me. It seems everyone I sponsor winds up with some sort of nickname, like Jitters, Waterfront Mac, Red John, Black John, Bad Attitude Benny, Depressed Danny, Valium Bob, and Bank Robber Beau.

I became real good friends with our local sheriff, who began letting guys out of jail for a few hours so I could take them to meetings—guys who are in the hoosegow for the same reason I was, drunk and disorderly. No one's escaped yet from "The Wet Brain Express."

Like I said, I always felt alone and afraid as a kid, but I've never felt that way since I sobered up in Alcoholics Anonymous. There was once a time when everything was always about me. Today I can actually put other people first and stop thinking that John is the most important guy on the planet.

That reminds me of a letter I received a few years ago from a young man who had heard me speak at an AA meeting in Seal Beach. The meeting just happened to be in Saint Ann's Catholic Church, where I made my First Holy Communion— after I ate that hellish peanut. The letter has come to mean a lot to me, and I'd like to close my story by sharing it with you. It reads:

> *Thank you for giving me your experience, strength, and hope at the Seal Beach meeting this past Monday. What a message you carry, John. I attend a small discussion meeting on Tuesday night and several people had also heard you at Seal Beach and were recalling things you had said.*
>
> *It was another Irishman alcoholic, Oscar Wilde, who said, "Life is far too important to be taken seriously." More than anything else in your pitch, the gift, and it is a gift, of your earthy and unexpected humor touched me.*
>
> *I appreciated very much the evident fact that you do what you do seriously—the Twelve Steps to recovery—*

but you don't take yourself seriously doing it. That's what I want!

Thanks for showing me how that can be done. I've not laughed that hard in a long time. May God hold you always in the palm of His hand, John. With my sincere and sober appreciation.

"I wanted what they had even though I didn't know what it was. It's called serenity."

THE STORY OF JOY P.

I was born in a little town in southern Manitoba, Canada, a place called Oak Lake, population about thirty-five. I was the youngest of three children. I had an older brother and an older sister.

When I was only eighteen months old, my father deserted the family. He was a turkey farmer. Apparently, he took his whole flock of turkeys into town one day and sold them, and then just disappeared. He left my mother all alone with three children and no money. I never knew whether he was an alcoholic or not.

While it was a real trial for my mother, she was a very strong woman and met her responsibilities as best she could. She had a good education, so she got a job as a country schoolteacher, working in different areas of southern Manitoba. Most of the children I grew up with were Ukrainian or Polish or Russian. As a result, I learned to speak many of their languages.

One Christmas, a Polish neighbor invited us to their home for dinner. Before the meal, they passed around a bottle of home brew. I was only nine at the time, but I knew there was liquor in the bottle and for some reason I couldn't wait to drink it. Why I wanted it so much I'll never know. If it were lemonade or Coke, I don't think I would have felt the same way. The fact that I knew it was alcohol seems to have created this desire in me.

However, when they passed the bottle to me and I started to pour myself a drink, one of the adults said, "No. Children do not drink this." So I handed the bottle to the next adult, feeling a bit resentful that I wasn't allowed to have at least one sip.

I decided I would volunteer to help clean up after dinner. I took some plates into the kitchen and then quickly grabbed the bottle of home brew, went into a pantry, and closed the door. I was all by myself. I poured what was left in the bottle into a tumbler and took a sip. It burned, but it went down into a place that made me feel very good. So I finished it. It was the first time in my life that I felt that good. I had a sense of peace that life seemed to be denying me. I had always felt alone. My mother was always teaching or was off with her new boyfriends, which left little time for her children.

But after drinking that tumbler of home brew, I felt loved. I felt warm and comfortable and at peace. And when I finished that tumbler, the only thing I wanted was more. However, when you're nine and weigh less than fifty pounds, a tumbler full of home brew is just too much. I got really drunk. I started to feel dizzy and sick, so I staggered outside. The temperatures in southern Manitoba at Christmastime run to forty degrees below zero. I reeled around and fell into a snowbank. Fortunately, one of the grandfathers at the dinner saw what happened, picked me up out of the snow, brought me back inside, and laid me on a couch.

I remember opening my eyes and seeing him looking at me with absolute pity. He said in his language, "Ona malenki piat," which translates into, "She is a little lush." If I had taken that as a warning, I might have saved myself a great deal of misery later on. But I didn't take it to heart.

We soon left that small country town and moved to Winnipeg, where I finished grade school and high school. In high school I became very friendly with a boy named Steve. One day he stopped me in the hallway and invited me to a party the following Saturday. He whispered that it was being held under a bridge between Winnipeg and St. Boniface. When I asked him why under a bridge, he said, "We'll have a lot of beer there, and since we're underage, we have to keep the party a secret." It sounded exciting, so I agreed to go.

Steve was right. They had plenty of beer at the party. He opened a bottle and handed it to me. I waited for him to hand me a glass, but he laughed and said everyone just drank it out of the bottle. I took a sip and thought it tasted terrible, so did the second. I asked Steve if he liked the beer, and he said he loved it. "From the very first taste?" I asked. "No," he said. "You have to develop a taste for it. It took me about six bottles."

I proceeded to drink six bottles myself, and you know, it worked like magic. I got to love beer. It became my drink of choice all through my drinking career. I came to love the taste, the smell, the size, the bubbles, the foam—everything about it. I just loved beer and what it did for me. That's why I wonder when I hear people say, "I needed to do something about my drinking problem, so I switched to beer." If it hadn't been for beer, I wouldn't have reached the bottom of my life, because that's where it took me for sure.

While I drank throughout high school and my two-year course at a business college, I did quite well in school. In fact, the business college hired me as their bookkeeper. But then World War II broke out, and I thought I should do something patriotic. I became a civilian bookkeeper for the Royal Canadian Ordinance Corps, a job I loved.

I found many people in the army I could drink with—privates, corporals, sergeants, and others. Most of them loved beer, and we had lots of time to drink together. One of the sergeants came to me one day, complaining that they didn't have any beer for the party they were having. He told me the commanding officer's Jeep was parked right downstairs with the keys in it. "Why don't you and I borrow it and get some beer?" he smiled. I went right along with him.

When we got back with a Jeep full of beer, the commanding officer was waiting for us. He said he could put both of us in jail for stealing government property. Instead he let us off with a severe warning never to touch the Jeep again.

A few days later, the commanding officer called me into his office. "Joy," he said, "I want to speak to you as a friend. Do something about your drinking before it ruins your life." I told him the only way I could stop was by getting away from all the people who made me drink so much. I asked him if he could possibly transfer me away from Winnipeg, and he promised to look into it.

Before the week was out, the commanding officer had me transferred to the headquarters of the Royal Canadian Ordinance Corps in Ottawa, and he gave me a good recommendation. I promised not to let him down. I also promised myself that not only was I going to stop drinking, I was also going to be an excellent employee, a good citizen, a good Christian, and a good person. I kept my promise not to drink for almost a year.

In Ottawa, I met a second lieutenant named Stan who also didn't drink. We began to date every Saturday night, going dancing or bowling or to a movie and never having a drink. Everything seemed wonderful. Liquor was rationed during the war, and people could only get one bottle each month. One day Stan's good friend Don, a heavy drinker, asked if we'd get a bottle each month and save it for him. So we did.

Since Stan expected to be sent overseas, he asked me to marry him before he went. I loved him and happily agreed. We then learned he wasn't shipping out for a while, so we moved into a second-story flat, where everything went well until one night when I had a very bad cold. I was really quite sick, and Stan suggested a good stiff drink might help. He reminded me that the liquor we had saved for his friend Don was still in our closet. It was a bottle of rum.

Stan mixed me a very strong rum and Coke. I took a big sip. It burned my throat but managed to stop on the way down at that sensitive spot that always made me feel so good. It was just like that first drink of home brew when I was nine years old. It gave me the same feeling—comfortable, happy, and carefree. I finished it and smiled at Stan. "I'm beginning to feel a little better. I think I'll have another."

Stan mixed me a second drink, and I mixed the third and the fourth and the fifth.

I didn't realize that one of the major symptoms of our disease had set right in. The first drink had set up the compulsion to drink more and more. I felt an uncontrollable compulsion to continue drinking to oblivion.

I don't remember falling asleep; I simply passed out. When I awoke, I noticed I hadn't even gotten undressed. Stan had gone off to the base, and the empty rum bottle lay at my side. It frightened me for a moment. I hadn't drunk since I left Winnipeg and now I drank more in one sitting than I could remember ever drinking before. My disease of alcoholism, which I knew nothing about, had progressed even though I hadn't drunk for a year. That's one of the terrible things about this disease—it continues to progress whether we're drinking or not.

So I made myself yet another promise: that I would never

drink again. "I will live the rest of my life without alcohol," I told myself, "because that is what I have to do."

The war ended, and Stan got a good job in Toronto as a chartered accountant.

We bought a lovely home, and I just knew everything was going to be wonderful in Toronto. I got pregnant and had a beautiful baby girl we named Sandra. I thought I was doing fine as a housekeeper and was a good wife and mother. My life seemed perfect since there was no liquor in the house, even though it often came to mind.

Then one evening my sister-in-law, Nancy, dropped by for a visit. She hadn't the slightest idea I ever had a problem drinking, so she brought a small gift for us to share—a case of Molson's beer tucked under her arm, my drink of choice. That's when something beyond my control took over. I just couldn't wait to get that case opened. And the beer inside was still ice cold, just the way I liked it. I yanked the top off one of the bottles and didn't even bother to pour it into a glass. I just tipped it up and guzzled it down.

At that moment in my life, beer just seemed to be the thing I needed to let me live and be comfortable with myself. Looking back, I realize that without alcohol I was really just managing to struggle through life. As soon as I had that drink of alcohol in me, I felt superhuman. I felt better than I had ever felt before.

My sister-in-law had no idea what her gift of beer initiated. It started me on ten years of daily, uncontrolled, compulsive drinking. I drank every single day. I spent housekeeping money on beer. When my housekeeping money ran out, I wrote my mother saying that my husband wasn't giving me enough money to live on and run the house. She began sending me something each week, having no idea I was drinking it away.

I was ashamed of my actions, but the compulsion to drink was stronger than my feelings of shame, so I continued to drink and was now losing everything important in life. I lost the love of my husband. He threatened to go to Children's Aid Society, declare me an unfit mother, and have my daughter taken away from me. While that really frightened me, I actually wound up pushing my daughter away from me myself.

One night I went into Sandra's bedroom to kiss her goodnight. As I bent over, she shoved me away from her, turned over on her side, and said, "Don't kiss me anymore, Mummy. You always smell of beer."

I went into the bathroom, closed the door, and literally fell on the floor weeping. I had never felt such guilt and shame before in my whole life. I was also filled with fear, since I realized I was helpless to stop my drinking. I had tried many things, but nothing worked. I had gone to my doctor and told him about my drinking problem; he gave me a prescription for some tranquilizers. That didn't help.

As my alcoholism progressed, I thought I was going crazy, so I went to see a psychiatrist. He said I was putting undue importance on alcohol. "You should treat it simply as a social grace in life," he told me. "Have a glass of wine with your dinner. It makes your dinner taste better. Have a cocktail in the evening or a little drink before you go to bed. It'll help you sleep better. That'll be sixty dollars, please." Needless to say, that didn't help either.

So I went to see my minister. After I told him my story, he wrote something on a piece of paper and handed it to me. It said, "I promise I will not take another drink as long as I live." He told me to sign it, take it home, and keep reading it to myself. I did, but each time I looked at it all I saw was a piece of paper. It didn't give me any strength at all. So I opened the fridge, took out a bottle of beer, and drank it.

My doctor, psychiatrist, and minister were all people who did good things in their own field, but I discovered that none of them could help a person with the threefold malady of alcoholism—something that affects us body, mind, and spirit. That's when I began to feel really hopeless.

A few days after my daughter pushed me away, my neighbor, a very kind lady named Jessie, knocked on my door. We hadn't been terribly close, but I was to discover that she knew more about me than I realized. I think most neighbors of us alcoholics do.

"I have something here that might be of interest to you," Jessie said, handing me a copy of the *Saturday Evening Post* containing a story by Jack Alexander about an organization called Alcoholics Anonymous.

Then she told me about a friend of hers named Eric who once drank uncontrollably. She said he lost his wife and family, got fired from a wonderful job, and wound up in very bad health, all the result of his drinking. She said he had become totally bankrupt in life. Then he found this fellowship called Alcoholics Anonymous and stopped drinking. It was like a miracle. Jessie said his life began coming together, his wife came back with the children, and he'd found a great position managing a resort hotel. Even his health was improving. "His life is totally restored since he joined Alcoholics Anonymous," Jessie said. Then she hugged me and left.

How my neighbor knew that I needed to hear all that and read the magazine story I couldn't figure out. But I read the story about AA and thought about all that had happened to Eric. It touched me. I considered calling Alcoholics Anonymous, but first I drank what liquor there was left in the house to get the courage. When I came to, I had a vague recollection I had made the call in a stupor and was worried I might have used bad language and insulted somebody. So I decided to call back.

A very kind lady answered the phone. I gave her my name, said I might have called the night before, and hoped I hadn't offended anyone. I could almost sense the smile on her face when she replied: "Yes, you did call, and I heard you were very nice. But you offered the man you spoke with fifty dollars to come over to your house and lock you up." I answered,

"That's the only way I'll ever stop drinking, if I'm locked up and forcibly kept away from it. If I'm free and at liberty, I will beg, borrow, and steal in order to get another drink. Please tell me what I can do."

The lady replied, "I can send someone out to talk with you or, if you think you're up to it, you can come down here and see me and we can talk about your problem."

I didn't want any strangers to see the way I was living, so I got washed and dressed, got on a bus, and went down to the AA office in downtown Toronto. I opened the door and saw a long flight of stairs facing me. As I started up the steps, I was suddenly filled with fear. I just felt so absolutely hopeless and helpless. I turned to leave. That's when I heard three words that I credit for saving my life.

I heard a lady's warm and loving voice say, "Welcome home, Joy." I turned back around and saw this lovely looking woman named Margaret standing at the top of the stairs holding out her hand. Something gave me the strength and willingness to climb the rest of the way up and grab her hand. I now know it was my Higher Power, whom I choose to call God. He used Margaret that day to save me from dying of alcoholism.

That was February 22, 1954, and I haven't had a drink since. AA has worked for me one day at a time by the grace of God.

Margaret, who I soon learned was the secretary at the Alcoholics Anonymous office, talked with me for a long time. Then she told me about a new AA group not far from where I lived and arranged for some people to take me there. So I went to my first meeting of the East York Group in Toronto in the basement of a Catholic church. There were two male members there with their wives, plus a few visitors. The men, Jim and Bill, were both alcoholics, and their wives, Betty and Jean, while not alcoholic were wonderful ladies who knew all about the AA program.

These four people took me under their wing and counseled

me. They never criticized me no matter what I said. They told me, "If you ever feel that you are in danger of taking a drink, pick up the telephone and call us. We'll always be there for you if you want to speak to us." They called it "the dime therapy" since phone calls were only a dime back then.

Right from the start I wanted what they had. I didn't know what it was, but they seemed to be at peace with themselves and with others, never struggling inside like I was. When I was finally able to understand, they said, "It's called serenity. It's a gift from God. Don't be impatient. Sometimes it takes some people a little longer to get. Just come to the meetings, don't drink, start working the Twelve Steps of recovery in your life, and thank God every day for your sobriety. That's all you have to do."

I faithfully did what they said each day, but I didn't seem to be getting close to what they had. I was sober about three months when one day I was crossing a busy street in Toronto. Something hit me halfway across the street. I remember the feeling and saying to myself, "I feel good. I feel at peace. I feel different. This is what they said is the gift from God—serenity." Then I stopped after crossing the street and murmured, "Dear God, I thank you for this priceless gift of serenity because today I really do feel at peace."

As I began to move ahead in the Twelve Steps of recovery, that gift of serenity grew even stronger. Since then, I have had this feeling of peace and the assurance that God is with me every day, even during the most difficult of times. That's because the promise came to me directly from God: I will never leave you or forsake you. And that's a promise that couldn't be broken. It's something I could always hang on to no matter what.

Sobriety has brought me many other gifts as well, including a son who was born a few years into my recovery when my husband and I started getting along a bit better. My son has never seen me take a drink, and together with my daughter, they are the joys in my life. But even in sobriety, we must face the problems that life brings. AA doesn't promise us that life will always be a bed of roses.

After thirty-two years of marriage, my husband, Stan, came to me one day and said, "You're no fun anymore. You've become a fanatic about sobriety. I've found somebody who's a little more like me, and I would like to have my freedom to pursue that relationship." He asked me for a divorce, and I felt like I was hit by a thunderbolt.

I was sober six years at the time and despite the pain, I decided you can't try to hang on to somebody who doesn't want you anymore. I said he could have his divorce, and I moved into my own apartment. It was very difficult at first since I didn't know how to handle life on my own. When I lived with my mother, she made all the decisions. When I married Stan, he made all the decisions. All of a sudden I'm all by myself trying to make my own decisions. But God was with me and helped me through it.

After a few months, Stan came by my apartment one day with the final divorce papers and asked me to sign them. I did. With my signature, I ended a thirty-two-year marriage. Stan put his arms around me and said, "I still love you, Joy, and I wish I had something of what you've found. But I don't." Then he hugged me and walked out of my life.

My heart was just absolutely breaking. I walked out on my fourth-floor balcony, looked down, and thought, "If I just lean over a little bit and hit that pavement below real hard, the hurting will stop." Then almost immediately I heard God telling me I could live through the pain. I still wasn't sure I could, so I went into the living room, knelt down, and cried out desperately to God for help. "Please God," I begged. "You have to help me through this. I don't know how to handle this on my own." Then I had a sense of God asking what I wanted him to do. "Let me hear my favorite hymn, 'Amazing Grace,' and I will take that as your promise to see me through this."

I got up and went into the kitchen to finish the dishes. My

little radio on the counter, which had been playing, suddenly went silent. As I reached over to find a new station, I heard a strong male voice singing "Amazing Grace." It was only minutes after asking God for this sign. I began to cry happy tears, for I now had absolute proof that prayers are heard and answered. Since that day I have always known that God will give me the strength to see me through difficult situations.

At times I've wondered whether I deserve this great gift of sobriety, since there's really nothing I've done to merit it. But the one thing I do know is that I can only keep it by trying to give it away. I do this by sharing my experience with newcomers every chance I get.

Every time I see newcomers at a meeting, I know the turmoil that's going on inside them. I take them by the hand and ask them to sit down and listen carefully to the stories of the people around them. This way they will surely come to realize that the program of Alcoholics Anonymous can do for them what it has done for so many others like myself. Then I say if they like what they see and hear, then stay—for it will be given to them, too, free of charge. All they have to do is be willing to try it.

I know today that anyone who truly seeks can find the wonderful peace and serenity that I have found in AA. I'm nobody special. Anyone can have it. All we have to do is ask God for his help. I believe that God is faithful. I just have to knock, and the door will be opened; seek, and I will find. It's just that simple, for God has always kept his promise. If I ask and knock, God will walk in and help me.

I remember, for example, the time Stan and I were traveling through the South. It was a hot, hot day in July. As we turned into this motel to spend the night, I noticed there was a liquor store next to it with a big sign outside reading, "Ice Cold Beer. Ice Cold Beer." When I went into that motel, all I could see was that sign, "Ice Cold Beer." I was sober about three years at the time and I remember telling myself I won't think about having a beer right now. I'll wait until we go into town and have dinner. If I still have the urge, I can always get a beer when we get back. I know now it was my disease talking to me.

On the way into town, we stopped at a red light. There was a bar on the corner. The door suddenly swung open, and a bouncer threw a drunken lady out into the street. She ended up right at my side of the car. I had the window down to get some air, so we came face-to-face. I could smell the beer on her breath. She glared at me, then cursed me and staggered off down the street. When the light turned green and we moved on, I thought to myself, "There but for the grace of God is where that beer would have brought me—just like that poor woman." Tears came to my eyes as I prayed for her, realizing at the same time how good God was to me.

That incident is something that has stayed with me all these years. It helps me realize what a dignified life I have in sobriety today. I have the respect of my friends, the love of my children, and respect for myself.

Recently my two children were visiting with me. It's always wonderful to be with them. As they were leaving, they told me again how proud they are of their sober mother and I told them how grateful I am for their love and caring. They and I know it's only because of this great gift of sobriety that God has given me that we are so close and loving today.

What a privilege and honor it is for me to share my story with others these days. I always hope that they can come to understand that what I have, they can have, too. All they need is the willingness to try, the willingness to ask the God of their understanding for help each morning and to thank their Higher Power for the help given each night. This way their sobriety, and the wonderful peace and serenity that come with it, will go on and on, one day at a time.

I'm eighty-nine years old now, and my gratitude for my sobriety continues to grow with each passing day.

"If we're willing to share all our garbage, we should be willing to share all the good stuff, too."

THE STORY OF MEL B.

I f you've ever read anything about the Roaring Twenties, well, it was supposed to have been a period of wild gaiety, heavy drinking, and slaphappy fun. That was the good-time era I was born into—September 9, 1925, to be exact, in a small town called Norfolk, Nebraska. But the only part of those so-called roaring good times that rubbed off on my DNA was the heavy drinking part. I missed out on the gaiety and slaphappy stuff.

In fact, I can remember being an unhappy, miserable little kid all the way back to the age of three. Okay, make that four. The simple truth is, I always felt different and uncomfortable in a crowd of more than one. While my older sister and younger brother were both very popular among their peers, I was an uncomfortable, depressing loner.

Of course, it didn't help that my parents were always

fighting and finally divorced when I was eleven. Not too many people got divorced back then, particularly in Norfolk, and I was so ashamed I tried to cover it up. When the kids at school and the people I knew in town would find out about it, I felt embarrassed and tried to avoid them.

I actually started drinking at a very young age. My father would let me have small glasses of wine, beer, and even whiskey sometimes. He believed that if you allow children to drink as they grew up, they would get used to it and not become alcoholics later in life. Boy, did I blow a hole in that theory.

That pattern of limited drinking continued right through grade school and into high school. But when there was an ample supply of booze around, like at parties and such, I usually overdid it. I think the first time I got really drunk was around fourteen, when I started high school. I got into my father's wine and suddenly learned how to create a million-dollar feeling.

At sixteen I dropped out of high school and spent about a year at various jobs in Denver and California. Then I joined the navy. It was May 1943 and World War II was raging. I thought I was being patriotic. The truth is, I really wanted to get away from all the trouble my drinking was getting me into. But as alcoholics soon discover, when we make that geographical change to get away from our problems, we always find the guy who created the problems right there when we arrive—ourselves. I think I crossed the invisible line into alcoholic drinking in the navy.

Even so, since it was wartime, I did my job in Uncle Sam's service quite well. I got through boot training at the U.S. Naval Training Station in Farragut, Idaho, and then navy diesel school on the campus of the University of Illinois. After additional training in San Diego and Hawaii, I served as a member of a small landing boat crew during the battle for Saipan. I was then transferred aboard USS *LST-555* for the initial assault on Anguar in the Palau Islands, Leyte and Lingayen Gulf in the Philippines, and on April 1, 1945, the landing on Okinawa, the last major campaign of World War II in the Pacific.

I was honorably discharged from the navy on November 8, 1946, with the rating of motor machinist's mate second class. Deep down, I knew how grateful I should have been that I wasn't court-martialed over my many drinking-related scrapes during my years of service. But, since most men in war drink or do other things, I guess it's hard to stand out too much from the crowd.

When I returned to Norfolk, my drinking continued. I leached off my mother and stepdad for a while, and then decided to stay with my father in Nampa, Idaho, near Boise. I found and lost several jobs due to my drinking and poor work habits. My drinking landed me in jail twice. My father and I argued a lot, and one day we had this real knock-down, drag-out affair. That's when I up and left for California, where I got a good job working in the oil fields near Ventura.

However, things went from bad to worse. I was getting drunk almost every day, and before the year was out, I had lost my job in the oil fields. I doubted I could find another job that paid enough to live on and drink on. I was now fast running out of money. I wanted to stop drinking, but didn't know how. I had tried all kinds of ways to stop, but once I picked up that first drink, all bets were off.

I had read about AA and even noticed its ad in the classified section of the Ventura newspaper. I also remembered reading a story about AA in a Boise newspaper when I was in jail. At the time I thought I was too young to be an alcoholic. This time things were really bad, so I decided to write a letter and sent it to the address listed in the ad.

Three days later I got a call from a man named Frank R. He came by my rooming house and took me to my first AA meeting in a nearby church basement. That was on October 7, 1948, and I had just turned twenty-three. There were ten other guys at the meeting, all much older than myself. One of them told me how lucky I was to be getting sober at such a young age.

I wish I could say that was the end of my drinking. I was greatly impressed by AA and the friendship I found there. I read the Big Book thoroughly and even memorized the Twelve Steps. After a month of attending four meetings weekly—all they had in the area—I went back to Idaho in the hope of building a better relationship with my father. It worked out badly, so I then went back to Norfolk for a short stay before returning to California. Jobless and discouraged in Los Angeles—but still sober—I got another bright idea that would lead to a very poor outcome.

Since I always had a warm bunk and three square meals a day in the military, I decided to enlist in the army. With no war on, I thought I'd sign up, get shipped overseas to some friendly European country, and have myself one big party. So in early 1949, I joined the United States Army. I lasted seven months. My drinking had me in and out of hospitals and finally in the guardhouse. One night, angry and very drunk, I set the guardhouse on fire. That did it. I was fortunate not to have been court-martialed and sent to prison for that move. I was simply kicked out of the army, this time with an undesirable discharge, all because of my alcoholic drinking.

I would like to note here that sixteen years later, through my recovery in Alcoholics Anonymous and the grace of God, some wonderful people, including a United States senator, helped me get my discharge upgraded to a general discharge. It was one more gift of sobriety.

After getting thrown out of the military with no place to go yet again, I decided to head for Norfolk, Nebraska, and sponge off my mother and stepfather one more time. Seven months later, I found myself locked up in the local Nebraska state mental asylum.

As I sat shaking and sweating in a dim, dank ward looking around at seriously mentally ill people, I began reflecting on my own life and wondering how I could have wound up in a place like this. To make it even worse, I recalled that when I was a young boy around nine, I and some of my—let's say dysfunctional—friends used to consider it great sport to ride our bikes out to "the nuthouse on the hill" and hoot derisive comments at shuffling groups of patients. Then we'd speed off, feeling like we had just taken a great risk daring to venture so close to "those crazy people." Now here I was, years later, one of them.

Back in 1935, I had been too young to know that the people we taunted were truly mentally ill, nor could I imagine that a variation of mental illness called alcoholism would someday bring me to this same place. And certainly there was no way I could have possibly conceived that my own future redemption was being carefully worked out during that same summer by two strangers in Akron, Ohio—Bill Wilson and Dr. Bob Smith.

Now April 15, 1950, it had been fifteen years since my nasty boyhood pranks. The world had changed drastically and so had I. I was not only one of those "shuffling crazy people" myself, but I had no confidence, no known goals, no firm principles, and hardly any friends. I knew nobody who had become such a complete failure in such a short period of time.

At this point I felt almost hopeless. I feared that frequent and long commitments to state hospitals would become the new norm of my life, as had other troubles. But what really disturbed me was the realization that I no longer had any control over my own life. I hated the life I was leading, but believed, to my despair, that I didn't have the power to change it. Despite my determination and many resolutions, I always seemed to drink again. Knowing now that each time I did I would wind up in an institution such as this, I became so despondent that I seriously considered killing myself. I had thought about this before in previous bouts of depression, but now I saw it as the only way out.

Then something remarkable happened. A day or two after this very dark and depressing night, while picking through a pile of books on the ward in an attempt to distract my mind, I found a stray copy of the book *Alcoholics Anonymous*. I remembered that I had read it before when I was going to those meetings in California, but I hadn't taken it seriously back then. I had never really accepted the idea that alcoholism is a permanent disease that a person is stuck with for the rest of his life. But now I had a different attitude, and the book made a great deal of sense to me.

I studied it almost every day and fought a savage battle with myself every time I started to rebel against some of its suggestions. It was fortunate, I believe, that AA urged only "willingness" instead of "action" on some of the tougher parts of the program, as I was hardly capable of decisive action at that point in my life.

I began attending AA meetings again, first at the hospital and then in town. At some point during the next seven weeks, I suddenly realized that I never had to drink again if I didn't want to. I was being given the tools of sobriety. It was almost unbelievable that one person could experience such a contrast of feelings during a hospital stay of less than two months. But that's the miracle of Alcoholics Anonymous. It was a true spiritual awakening, for I haven't had a drink since April 15, 1950, and my life steadily improved.

Many of the older AA members I met at that time were more skeptical about the prospects of younger alcoholics than they are today. "You've got a tough fight ahead of you," one gray-haired gent said. "You'll be really lucky if you get the program at your age," remarked another man with a bald head and a beard. Even an elderly fellow who never lost a job or thought about committing suicide or was ejected from the army in disgrace patted me on the head saying how glad he was I could avoid all the suffering he'd endured if I managed to stay sober!

All these well-intended remarks were valuable, for they helped me see that I was a bit different from some other AA members. I was far more unstable, and my emotional development had been so retarded that I hadn't even acquired the simple social skills other people take for granted. "Mel has to learn about everything," one of my friends was to say a few years later, and he was right. And even at that late date, he was making such a remark to excuse crude behavior that I hadn't as yet corrected.

So pain and humiliation continued long after my last drunk, but this was the pain and humiliation of the growing-up process. It eventually brought the pleasure of achievement, and as I look back down the road I've traveled since then, I wonder how long it takes most people to realize what marvelous changes can be made in a human life through following the program and living the Twelve Steps. Today I am absolutely certain that "with God all things are possible."

I first became aware of the tremendous, continuing assistance available from a Higher Power when I realized that something beyond myself was removing the baffling compulsion to drink. As practical results developed, I began to respect the practical side of living a spiritual life. I discovered that God's help is not limited to my drinking problem alone, but extends into all phases of my life.

But then I made a serious misstep. Somehow, since I had found an immediate answer for my drinking problem, I concluded that answers for all of my problems should also come so swiftly—for anything that might be disturbing me at the moment and for things I thought would make my life better. So I began offering up prayers for assistance, like a little child making out a Christmas list for Santa Claus. When I soon learned that God doesn't readily meet all my requests and demands, I became a little miffed.

My agitation increased even more as I looked around the rooms of AA and saw others with many of the advantages I wanted for myself. Worse yet, I would see people I felt weren't living on a "spiritual basis" like I was but were still enjoying an outpouring of luck in all directions. I thought I was doing my best to be moral, kind, courteous, helpful, and honest. Why shouldn't good things be coming my way, too, even some of those nice material things?

With feelings of resentment building inside of me, I reluctantly decided to discuss it with a sponsor. He was very kind and told me that I should stop judging other people and taking their inventories. Then he explained that this type of thinking could lead me into blind alleys of self-pity, feeling that God was cheating me. He said I needed to go back to the Third Step and then start working hard on the Eleventh Step—to commit myself completely to God's will whatever it is and regardless of the consequences. He reminded me again that acceptance of God's will is the key to my serenity and my success at living a sober life. I followed his advice and that's when things began to change—and I gradually received that peace of mind I so desperately wanted.

I had some relatives in Pontiac, Michigan, who owned a machine shop. I went back there in September and they hired me on. Six months later, I landed a job on the assembly line at Detroit Diesel. I went to AA meetings every night in Detroit and made some friendships that would last for more than thirty years. After fifteen months at the diesel engine plant, I joined the purchasing department of Aeroquip Corporation, a manufacturer of aircraft and industrial products in Jackson, Michigan. After several months in purchasing, I worked in production control for three years.

For some reason, God had blessed me with a flair for writing, something I've always enjoyed doing. Through my good fortune, after writing a few articles for Aeroquip's company magazine, I was assigned to write and produce the publication myself. Then my duties with management continued to expand, and in 1956 I became the firm's public relations representative. I wrote press releases, speeches for company officials, stories for the company publication, and business articles for industry magazines. Aeroquip was eventually merged with Libbey-Owens-Ford Company, where I also worked in public relations until retiring in 1986. I share all this because, looking back, I was now simply trying to follow the will of my Higher Power.

Another area of my life in which God guided me was in improving my education. I felt some shame and a bit of low self-esteem for dropping out of high school when I was sixteen. I finally received my high school diploma in 1967. A few months later I decided to enter college, attending mostly night classes, since I was working. I'm pleased to report that with God's help and support from a very patient wife, I graduated cum laude from the University of Toledo in 1975.

I came to discover that sobriety affords one the tremendous freedom to do many things and unleashes the talent God has given us to accomplish them. So, in addition to graduating from college and writing business articles, I started writing stories for AA's *Grapevine* magazine, many of which were published over the years. I've also written a number of books on recovery. But perhaps the greatest privilege God has given me in this area of my life was to help write our cofounder Bill Wilson's biography, called *Pass It On*, which was published in 1984 by Alcoholics Anonymous.

Another activity I came to enjoy with my freedom from booze was acting in community theater. There was a good one in Jackson, Michigan, where I lived and worked for a time, and they seemed to like my hamming it up on stage. I participated in more than twenty-five plays, taking on leading roles in *Mr. Roberts, The Caine Mutiny, South Pacific,* and *My Fair Lady,* among others.

One day at the start of rehearsals for *The Great Sebastians,* I met an attractive young lady named Loraine ("Lori"). We hit it off right away and were soon engaged. It was early 1960, and I had been sober almost ten years. Lori was an artist and did fashion drawings for an upscale retail chain. She was volunteering her time and talent to do drawings for our play. I was blessed that she not only fell in love with me but also with AA. We began going to meetings together on a regular basis, and in September 1960 we got married. Today we have three wonderful sons, Wayne, Craig, and Dean, a lovely daughter, Lynne, and nine beautiful grandchildren ages three months to twenty-five years.

I've shared with you a lot of the good things that have happened to me in sobriety, along with the bad things that occurred when I was drinking. That's what I do when offered the opportunity to speak at an AA meeting. I was told a long time ago that if I'm willing to share all my garbage, then I should be willing to share all the good stuff, too. Newcomers in particular need to hear how this program works to better our lives.

But sometimes when you share the good stuff, some people take this as flaunting your ego, that you're bragging instead of eating humble pie. I say nonsense—that "ego" is not always "bad." For example, it's not altogether bad to have some self-assertive, self-preserving tendencies or even to pat yourself lightly on the back once in a while and think you're just a little bit special. These tendencies, which were obviously liabilities when we were drinking, can be an asset in some ways when we're sober. I know I probably have the "AA ego police" jumping up and down right now, but I'll continue speaking my piece, anyway.

Where else but in Alcoholics Anonymous can a once down-and-out bum like me become an occasional speaker who shares the great miracle of his recovery? Is that bad? Where but in our fellowship can a born loser find himself sharing bottle-hiding experiences with country club dropouts? Is that bad? And who else gives a battered outcast an opportunity to turn his sordid past into valuable AA currency but fellow members of this unique program? Is that also bad?

It seems to me that despite our shortcomings, most of us coming into AA need ego deflation about as much as we need another hangover. We've already been cut down to size hundreds of times by judges, employers, police officers, bartenders, and angry spouses, and even by our own sick images staring back at us from a filthy bathroom mirror in some fleabag hotel. We need to start feeling better about ourselves.

That's why I think this overpopularized idea of AA being an ego-deflating outfit is a bit overblown. A good sponsor can usually do the ego-trimming job that might be necessary and do it quite well by sharing his own experience. But putting people like us through another tough ego-deflating process seems like a bit of overkill.

I also believe that holding back and not sharing the good things that happen as a result of working the Twelve Steps and through the grace of God can often be false humility. We can be so prideful that we want everybody to see us as this quiet, humble little guy. I personally believe it's selfish not to let others know all about the good things that happen to us in AA. So if you're willing to share all your garbage with us, then start sharing all the good stuff, too.

I don't want to beat this horse to death, but I do have one more point to make on this subject. Despite my belief in the need for a healthy ego, I think it's a mistake to believe that the ego can no longer cause any trouble simply because a person has stopped drinking. I've seen situations where some people think they've become overly important members of their AA group and know what's best for the rest of us members. That's when I've seen egos collide and cause serious trouble in the group. But I believe if we work on AA's Twelve Traditions as hard as we need to work on AA's Twelve Steps, we can divert such ego clashes and any other ego problems in our lives.

Through my AA activities over the years, I've had the good fortune to meet and hear our late cofounder Bill Wilson speak many times and to get to know him personally as a very warm, wise, and cordial man. I missed meeting Dr. Bob Smith, our other cofounder, because he passed away shortly after I sobered up. I would like to close my story by describing the very first time I met Bill for real conversation. It was at a symbolic time and place, and I will always be grateful that I had the opportunity to take his photo that day, a special photo that has come to mean so much to me.

It was June 15, 1958, and it was Founders Day for AA in Akron, Ohio. Bill was at the gravesites of Dr. Bob and his wife, Anne Smith, where he would deliver a brief memorial message. As I looked around on this golden bright Sunday morning, I thought how appropriate it was that it was also Father's Day and that the crowd of people gathered here for this simple memorial service must have strong feelings about these two fine men who were the human fathers of Alcoholics Anonymous.

I had met Bill quite by chance an hour earlier in the coffee shop of the Mayflower Hotel in Akron, where he recognized the group I was with as members of AA. Then, as comfortable as an old shoe, he sat down at our table and had breakfast with us. He told us a great deal about his hopes for AA and his belief that, with Dr. Bob gone, the fellowship needed to take a stronger hand in looking out for itself. He said that at this point, AA no longer needed any special help from him other than occasional advice and the services that he might be able to give as a result of his experience.

Bill said his principal concern now was to help AA's *Grapevine* magazine, the program's "meeting in print," become a more effective medium of communications throughout the fellowship. This was a goal I certainly believe he met before passing away in 1971.

It occurs to me now, some fifty-two years later, that Bill had by 1958 moved gracefully into the role of AA elder statesman. He was deliberately taking steps to guard against becoming a "bleeding deacon," the type of older member who attempts to dominate the fellowship and to block any change not of his own making. Bill always admitted that he had many of the character traits of the bleeding deacon, so he made a conscious effort to avoid becoming such a person.

At the second International AA Conference in 1955, for example, he had gone so far as to make a formal and symbolic statement that effectively assigned responsibility for AA to the members and their elected delegates. He wanted AA to be a fellowship that could easily get along without him.

I also knew from people very close to Bill that he was finally making progress in overcoming severe mental depression that had plagued him since the early 1940s. He still had problems, of course, but at breakfast that morning at the Mayflower Hotel he told us that a committed and frequent course of strenuous walking seemed to greatly improve his moods. Still, he admitted he was not always as serene and energetic as he'd like to be. In fact, that very afternoon found him in a state of fatigue following his talk before fifteen hundred AA members and other friends celebrating Founders Day at the University of Akron fieldhouse.

I cannot remember much of what Bill said that morning at the memorial service other than that he walked over to the gravestone and simply began talking to Dr. Bob and Anne as if they were present. I think he talked about the accomplishments of Alcoholics Anonymous and our efforts as members to meet the high standards they had set for us years ago. There was great sincerity in Bill's words and manner, and I now think that he did feel he was in direct communication with these two wonderful people, wherever they were.

Bill truly believed in everlasting life, without defining it or attempting to explain just how it works. I am sure he believed that Bob and Anne were living somewhere out there in the Eternal Goodness or, as many in our fellowship like to say, at "that great big AA meeting in the sky."

When Bill closed the memorial service by placing a large wreath at the headstone, he asked all of us to join him in silence. As we bowed our heads, a church bell nearby began sounding, so perfectly timed with our service that one lady let out a short gasp of wonder. Then we said the Lord's Prayer together, making us all feel that this short memorial service had really been another AA meeting.

There were only thirty or forty people at the 1958 service, the first ever held at the gravesite. Twenty years later, in 1978, the crowd at the gravesite was much larger. Many people came out to the cemetery in a motorcade led by motorcycle patrolmen. Dr. Bob would have had his misgivings about that, since he was a modest man who did not like to be the subject of any special honors or memorials. Bill would have had some misgivings, too, but he would have accepted our desire for such a service as part of the group conscience. Bill and Bob were both great examples of what an AA elder statesman should be.

I took a picture of Bill that day at the memorial service that I've shared with many of my AA friends all over the world. I have a framed copy of it standing on the desk in my home office. It is a constant reminder of how all this started and how it saved my life that day at the Norfolk, Nebraska, state mental asylum. I plan to continue carrying the message Bill and Dr. Bob passed on to us wherever I go and for however long I have remaining on this earth—enjoying this wonderful life of sobriety.

*"My mother never reported me missing.
She knew I'd come home once I could no
longer buy, beg, borrow, or steal liquor."*

THE STORY OF MILLIE W.

The fellowship of Alcoholics Anonymous was less than a dozen years old when I first stuck my perky Irish nose under its tent. It was 1947 and I hadn't quite turned twenty-one. I sure wish I could have stayed, but this insidious disease of alcoholism had me firmly in its grip.

I was also on the verge of my second divorce and was living with my parents, my sisters, and the son I had from my first marriage. Now, I wouldn't call these rather shaky unions real marriages between two people who honestly cared for each other. I'd describe them instead as legitimized affairs between two people who liked to drink and get drunk together.

Both of my parents drank a lot when I was growing up, but my father was the raging alcoholic. My mother, whom he abused terribly, always tried to control her drinking to be there for her children. I certainly didn't want to be like my father, so I didn't have anything to drink until I was almost out of high school. But I did have a hidden wild streak in me, and boy, did it ever burst forth at my high school prom. That's where I started to drink; I don't even remember whether I got home that night or sometime the next day.

Looking back, I can clearly see that once I picked up that first drink, I just couldn't put it down. I started drinking shortly after I turned eighteen, and by the time I was twenty-one, I was a full-fledged alcoholic.

In addition to having a wild streak, I was a very angry person. My home life was very dysfunctional, to say the least. On top of that, I had been raped by a cousin's husband when I was fourteen, and nobody did anything about it. So I went from a very angry, mixed-up person as a teenager to a very angry, mixed-up alcoholic as a young woman. I would get a job and lose it, then get another job and lose that. My life always seemed to be in turmoil.

I never liked to drink at home. I loved the taprooms. That's where all the fun and excitement was, and I enjoyed being admired and chased by all the men. For a while it helped lift my low self-esteem—that is, until I began waking up in cheap motel rooms with strangers, realizing what I had done the night before.

My mother would always try to talk to me when I'd come home after a two- or three-day drinking spree. She never reported me missing. She knew I'd be home once I could no longer buy, beg, borrow, or steal any more liquor. She'd tell me what a lousy mother I was to my son and how I was becoming something I swore I would never be—the exact image of my alcoholic father. We'd scream at each other, then I'd stagger into my bedroom to sleep it off. Sometimes I'd be sick as a dog, but as soon as I felt a little better I'd head back to those taprooms.

There was a lady down the street from us named Mrs. Riley who had a brother in Alcoholics Anonymous, something I had never heard anything about. My mother would talk to this lady about me, telling her how frightened she was that someday I'd be found dead in the street or in some back alley. Mrs. Riley said, "Why don't you bring your daughter to AA? It saved my brother's life." Then she told my mother about this AA clubhouse at 4021 Walnut Street, which was just across town.

So one day when I came home really sick and very down, my mother said to me very calmly that she wanted me to go with her to see some people who can help me straighten out—and if I didn't go with her, she'd take my son away from me and never let me back into the house. Since she caught me at a very weak moment—I was not only sick but broke—I agreed to go with her to this clubhouse.

I'll never forget walking into that place with my mother dragging me by the arm. It was like a mansion. It had a large center hall with two beautiful parlors on each side, one of them with this gorgeous piano in it. I was really impressed. I learned the house was owned by a very wealthy man who had gotten sober in AA and turned it into a clubhouse for AA meetings as well as to help drunks dry out and have a place to hang around. We walked into one of the parlors, where I was shocked to see some of the oldest men I'd ever seen in my life. Some of them had scraggily white beards and blue veins popping out of their fat, red noses.

As my mother led me toward them, I noticed they were staring at me like I was some kind of a nut, which I probably was at that time. While I wasn't all that bad-looking if I must say so myself, I was skinny and malnourished from eating pretzels dunked in beer for breakfast. My mother dragged me up to one man who appeared somewhat well-dressed and sternly sober, and she said rather loudly, "This is my daughter. You've got to help her stop drinking. She drinks all the time, and you have to help her to stop or she'll die."

That's when I saw the looks on the faces of these men

soften. Some of them smiled at me rather warmly. They invited us to sit and have coffee with them. I remember there was a bar in the parlor with a large coffee urn on top and a bunch of coffee mugs next to it. The well-dressed man began to tell me about himself and what had happened to his life because of his drinking. Then some others chimed in.

I really don't remember much of what they said that day because I was a little scared and very bewildered, especially about the thought of never drinking again. But then I said to myself, If I do come here for a while, maybe my mother will get off my back, not threaten to take my son away, and let me keep living off her at the house. My motives were completely selfish, and I was convinced I could put one over on everyone here, including my mother—for a while, anyway.

So I gritted my teeth, stopped drinking, and started going to the AA clubhouse a few days a week. I had no idea what it was all about, and I cared less. All I knew was that the static at home had stopped and I was beginning to feel better than I had in some time. I was also meeting some interesting people—mostly men. There was this very wealthy guy who took me out on his big boat a few times. He treated me wonderfully, but I always thought that sailing on a boat and drinking went hand in hand. At this point the desire to drink was still with me, and I was missing the taprooms. Since this wealthy guy had no booze on his big boat, the relationship went nowhere.

Then I met a chemist who was very well educated. He was much older than me and walked with a cane. When he found out I was getting a divorce from my second husband, he asked me to move in with him so he could teach me how to stay sober. I've since learned that's called "Thirteenth Stepping."

There weren't many women in Alcoholics Anonymous back then, but I did meet one at the clubhouse. Her name was Jo S. She's since passed away. She became my first AA sponsor some years later, but I didn't like her at all when we first met. Jo was a former marine and acted like she was still in the service, always speaking tough and giving orders. She told me to stay away from the men if I really wanted to stay sober. Since I knew in my head that I didn't want to stop drinking—not right then and there, anyway—I paid little attention to her during my first go-round in the program.

I had been attending meetings for some weeks, but all I was really doing was coasting until the heat at home cooled down. I kept telling my mother about all the fine people I was meeting, how nice they were to me, and how much they were helping me. But all the while I was planning my next safari.

My twenty-first birthday was approaching. I told my mother I'd be celebrating it with some friends at the AA clubhouse. It was a bold-faced lie. I got all dressed up, but instead of heading to Walnut Street, I went straight to a taproom in a very bad section of Philadelphia where I thought no one would know me and word that I was drinking again wouldn't get back to my mother.

How dumb we alcoholics can be, thinking we can somehow hide our disease from the world. All I remember of that night was getting very drunk, saying something very nasty to the bartender, and then getting into a fight with his big, fat girlfriend. She picked me up bodily and threw me out the front door. I landed in the gutter, all dressed up and celebrating my twenty-first birthday as drunks like me usually do.

The next four years were the worst of my drinking years. I'd leave the house, promising again to go to an AA meeting, and come back a few weeks or a month later all beat up, with teeth missing and two black eyes. While my mother was raising my son, I'd be out roaming the streets clutching a small brown paper bag that held all my belongings—a comb and brush, lipstick and eye makeup, a toothbrush, and hair spray. Despite all the humiliation from my drinking, I was still quite vain and egotistical. My defenses were always up, supported by the enormous denial of my disease.

It got so bad at one point that I finally begged my mother

to let me come home one last time and try to straighten myself out. Although she had little hope left, she still loved me and carried her own guilt for what I went through as a child. So I came back, cleaned up, went back to AA, met a nice man of my own Catholic faith and Irish nationality, and married him in a Catholic church. I thought I had it made. We had a beautiful little daughter, and then we had one huge argument. I stormed out of his life and out of AA once again and got drunk—a drunk that lasted five more years and cost me yet another marriage, ill health, and the loss of my self-respect.

Now with two children, I decided I would hold things together by controlling my drinking. Have you ever heard of controlled drinking working for any alcoholic? Well, it didn't work for me, that's for sure. I was back again living with my mother, and before I knew it, I had bottles hidden all over her house.

One morning when my mother was gone and I couldn't find any of my hidden bottles, I called a babysitter and went out. I headed to a taproom, got very drunk, staggered outside, and collapsed in the street. Someone must have called the police, because the next thing I knew, I came to strapped to a table in a hospital with doctors and nurses staring down at me. I didn't know my name or who I was. I do remember, however, that the straps were so thick and tight on my arms and legs that they frightened me. I thought I'd never be let loose.

I came home about a week later. I told my mother that after such an experience, I was sure I would never drink again. But when I looked at the sadness on the faces of my son and daughter and thought about all the hurt I was causing them and everyone around me, I knew I would either drink again or kill myself.

That night I searched the house and found a bottle I had hidden in a closet. I went into the bathroom and without any hesitation and despite all that had happened to me, I put it to my lips and drank. I drank the whole thing. Then I stared long and hard into the large mirror on the medicine cabinet. I hated what was staring back. I threw the empty bottle at the mirror. Glass flew all over the bathroom. The last thing I remember is crawling across all that broken glass to the toilet bowl. My mother came rushing in to find me spitting up blood, with my hands and arms badly cut. She called an ambulance.

That first night back in the hospital, I knew I had hit my bottom. I made a decision to turn my life and my will over to the care of God. I knew he was my only hope. This time when I came out, I went straight to 4021 Walnut Street. Everyone there at the AA clubhouse embraced me, and that's where I started a whole new life—on August 2, 1956.

Jo S., the former marine, was still there. She was married now and had two children. She simply smiled at me and said, "I knew you'd be back someday." As I said, Jo became my first AA sponsor; she guided me through the Steps and the principles of this marvelous program until the day she died. Jo was close friends with another great AA member, a man named Tom S., who had founded the Westinghouse Group in Eddington, Pennsylvania, which wasn't that far away. I learned a lot from Tom, as well. He told me early on that no matter how many bad decisions or bad choices I had made, if I stayed close to God and didn't pick up a drink, I'd be okay.

One of the things I'll never forget was the day a bunch of us were sitting around the clubhouse chatting after a meeting when a radio report announced that the American Medical Association had accepted alcoholism as a disease that required treatment. I think it was around the spring of 1956, because I hadn't been sober a year yet. Everybody cheered, I guess because alcoholics and others could no longer be skeptical about the claim AA had always made that alcoholism was a disease.

On Saturday nights at the clubhouse we would play Bingo.

There was a man named Tom D., who would call the numbers. He'd always get hooted at by people waiting for him to call a particular number so they could yell "Bingo!" But he'd hoot right back. A lot of people would bring food and desserts, and we'd have a grand old time. In the beginning, it was this kind of fellowship that made me want to come back to more and more meetings; I just wanted to be with these kind and loving people.

Because I still had the shakes for a while, Jo would bring me to Philadelphia General Hospital every few days to get a vitamin B-12 shot. Back then, many people in AA believed this helped calm the nerves and relieve anxiety. The shot cost a dollar, but if you couldn't afford it they'd give it to you anyway. You don't hear about people taking vitamin B-12 much anymore.

I have many wonderful memories of so many wonderful friends I made in AA over the years and all they did for me. Many of them have long since passed, but the memories of them and how much they helped me will never fade.

I married again in sobriety, to a kind and caring Polish man named Zigman. I was in my forties and had been sober almost fifteen years. I had known him and his wife for some time. I was impressed at how loving he always was to her, especially when she became seriously ill. He rarely left her bedside until she finally passed away.

After a while we began to date. I still had some anger inside because my life wasn't going the way I wanted it to go. Zigman, who had nine years more sobriety than I, helped me a lot by suggesting I work harder on my spiritual life and turn things over to the care of God. When we got married, we would have our own little AA meeting over breakfast each morning, reading from the Big Book or from some spiritual literature. What a wonderful way to start the day. My husband died eleven years ago. He was a very strong and good man, and I still miss him very much.

One day I started coughing. It would come and go, so it

didn't worry me. But then it turned into a hacking cough. I didn't want to take any cough medicine because back then, most cough syrups contained alcohol. But it gradually got worse and began to concern me. When I went to see the doctor, he thought at first it was a cold that was hanging on and prescribed antibiotics. When the cough didn't go away, he decided it must be allergies. Finally, when the cough came back worse than before, he sent me to the hospital for some extensive tests. They discovered I had lung cancer and had to remove one of my lungs. About a year after that I had a heart attack. Neither time did I even think about picking up a drink.

Ever since I came back to Alcoholics Anonymous more than fifty-three years ago, I've always made sure that every time I go see a doctor or go into a hospital, the first thing I say is, "I'm an alcoholic and I can't take anything with alcohol in it or anything that could mess up my head and lead me back to drinking." I do this because I want to be a sober woman today, and the AA program is my life. I try to live it to the best of my ability each and every day and carry its great message to others.

During those times when I was recuperating, my sponsor Jo would bring some ladies from our group over to my house, and we'd have an AA meeting. Then when I got well, I continued to invite women over for a meeting, especially the younger women. I guess I felt I had something special to share with them, since I became an alcoholic at such a young age.

Even though I'm now eighty-three years old and quite disabled, I still carry the message in any way I can—on the phone, writing letters, and in the AA meetings I have here at my house twice a month with other ladies in the fellowship. While I have a bad heart condition and have to be on oxygen twenty-four hours a day, I'm still alive and kicking and won't stop working this marvelous program until I'm taken to that big AA meeting in God's house.

When I was operated on for lung cancer seventeen years

ago, I was sent home to die. But I'm still here, so I guess God wants me to continue doing what I'm doing. And I still keep one hand in God's hand and the other in the hands of Alcoholics Anonymous so I don't have a hand left to drink with. How grateful I am to be in such a position today.

"I've been making geographical changes since the day I was born—until I finally found a permanent home in Alcoholics Anonymous."

THE STORY OF OTTO W.

I think I inherited the itch in my britches from my father, who was always chasing another dream—a dream that always told him, "It will be much better once I get there...," wherever "there" was. Every time I got into trouble drinking, I would say the same thing. But it never was any better.

It goes without saying that my father also drank a lot. So did my mom. They met and married in Canada and immigrated to Pontiac, Michigan, where my older brother and I were born. I made my appearance on August 22, 1930, just as the Great Depression was getting under way in America. My parents were European—Irish and Swiss—and they truly lived by the motto "Spare the rod, spoil the child."

My folks are gone now; alcohol played a significant part in both of their deaths. I do believe that their history would have been mine except for the intervention of God as I understand him and the program of Alcoholics Anonymous.

My formative years were spent crisscrossing the country, moving every time my dad got a whim that there was something better right around the corner. We moved from Michigan to California, then to Oregon, and back to California. We settled in to Dawson Creek, Canada, just north of Calgary for a while; then it was back to California for another year or so before giving Michigan another try and then again back to California. I had a very difficult time connecting with other kids, since I never knew when I would come home from school to see the car being loaded for another geographic.

I don't know if this had anything to do with my becoming an alcoholic, but it sure contributed to feelings of low self-esteem, loneliness, anger, and fear. While I was soon to follow in my parents' footsteps and take up drinking to ease the pain, my older brother took a different direction with his life. He threw himself into schoolwork wherever we were and eventually became a very successful businessman. He was to bail me out of many jams—physically, financially, and emotionally—over my drinking years.

My mother battled her problems with alcohol by going to church. She was a devout Roman Catholic, and we attended Mass and received the sacraments regularly. It seemed to sit well with my brother, who remained a steadfast Catholic all his life. I, on the other hand, was a true doubting Thomas and wasn't able to experience God on any level until I finally came into Alcoholics Anonymous and got sober on August 20, 1959. With God's help and the Twelve Steps of AA, I never had to take another drink. But it took a lot of pain and suffering to get there.

We were living in Canada when the Second World War broke out. With all the able-bodied men being called into service, there were plenty of job opportunities around for us younger fellows. I was fourteen at the time and hired out to work the area farms during the summer. We kids worked just as hard as the older guys and were treated just the same. We toiled all week and went to town on Sundays, where we drank alongside the older men we farmed with. No one thought anything about it. At this young age, I discovered the relief alcohol can bring. Loneliness and fear vanished. I felt part of the world at last.

At seventeen, I joined what was back then called the U.S. Army Air Force. After basic training, I was shipped off to Alaska. I'll never forget celebrating my eighteenth birthday there with a Yaqui Indian named Guillermo. We bought two fifths of tequila and two fifths of whiskey. It turned out that Guillermo and I were the only ones at my birthday party and still we ran out of booze. I wound up at the base infirmary after going on the warpath at the Mecca Bar & Grill with my Yaqui buddy and coming out the big loser. This was to be an omen of the progression of my alcoholism.

In 1950 I was sent to Fort Bragg in North Carolina, where I was assigned to a special communications unit bound for Korea. I was in combat for eighteen months, including two brief trips to Japan, where I was treated for shrapnel wounds and sent right back to the front. Since I used all the will-power at my command to stay away from booze in Korea so I wouldn't endanger my buddies, I let it all hang out during those few weeks of treatment in Japan. I stayed drunk the whole time I was there.

When I returned to the States in March of 1952, my drinking quickly got out of control. My frequent attempts to stop or even slow down were for naught. The Air Force thought my behavior was the result of traumatic experiences in Korea and tried to figure out what to do with me while I was supposedly working my way back to sanity. They finally decided to send me—or sentence me—to head up communications on Grand Turk Island in the Bahamas.

Grand Turk is a very small island in a lush tropical paradise, the kind of place most alcoholics would love to spend their lives, provided they had an ample supply of booze. Also, one would think it would be difficult to get into too much trouble on such a small patch of sand in the middle of a large blue ocean. My out-of-control alcoholism quickly proved that theory wrong. I found a heck of a lot of trouble from the moment I arrived until the moment they handcuffed me and sent me back to the States.

Since Grand Turk was pretty "dry" when I arrived, I immediately got into the whiskey business. I paid some fellow Air Force buddies to fly in cases of top-shelf booze from the States and peddled them throughout the Bahamas, keeping plenty for myself, of course. The colonel in charge heard some rumors about what was going on and fingered one of the guys working with me. He threatened to court-martial him unless he snitched on everyone. That lit my drunken fuse. I got into a raging argument with the colonel and wound up pushing him around until he finally ran off to get some help.

The "troops" were called in and I took off in a boat loaded with whiskey. I had no idea where I was headed, probably for another island. But they came after me in a faster boat and a seaplane, finally cornering me and putting me in chains.

Instead of throwing me immediately into the brig, a senior officer who knew some of my history sent me off to a military rehab in Florida. A few days later I was transferred to a neuropsychiatric hospital at Maxwell Field in Alabama. There I was diagnosed with "chronic alcoholism and emotional immaturity." It was a diagnosis I hated but managed to live up to for the next six years. After another series of drunken episodes, the air force finally decided to discharge me from the service for chronic alcoholism but gave me an honorable discharge.

Returning home, I decided to make one more attempt to change my life for the better. I entered college on the GI Bill and for a short time did pretty well with the business of living—trying to control my alcohol intake and focus on my studies. While I was a good student and held a steady job for a while, my attendance at both school and work eventually became a problem. Employers should never pay drunks on Thursday if they expect them to show up on Friday. Once again, alcohol ended any run of success I might have had.

Soon I found myself living the life my father lived, a life I once hated. Now my own geographics began—another move, another failure. Surely it will be better there, I'd tell myself, because this time I won't drink so much when I get there. The trouble was, when I got there, the drunken Otto was there, too.

Some time in mid-1956 I wound up in the Lynwood city jail in California for drunk walking, a polite way of saying public intoxication. Here, I got to talking with Pat, one of my newer drinking buddies and cell mate, about quitting this merry-go-round of drunk and jail, drunk and jail, drunk and jail. So as we alcoholics do, we conjured up an innovative plan. We decided to become lumberjacks in Oregon. We were determined to get healthy there, meet a few good women, settle down, and live a good life.

Upon my release the next day, I took Pat home with me to help me pack for our trip. My parents were so delighted to see me go, they helped us pack up the car. On the way out of town, Pat and I stopped at the Red, White, and Blue liquor store and bought just one small pint of whiskey to christen our new venture.

One year later I found myself alone and drunk in Santa Barbara, a distance of only 108 miles from our starting point. I had lost track of Pat somewhere along the line. I knew I needed a new plan, and for some reason, my whiskey-soaked brain told me that Las Vegas was the place for me to sober up. Naturally, it turned out to be one more failed geographic.

During my first three months in Las Vegas, I managed not to drink. This brief period of sobriety convinced me that I was now back in control. I worked as a busboy at one of the larger hotels and had to pass the casino bar on my way to work. One morning I stopped at the bar and ordered a double shot. I threw it down and asked for another. I never made it to work that day, that week, or ever again. I was now completely out of control. Seven days later I found myself walking out of Vegas, a pony of wine stuck in the front of my trousers.

Broke, sick, and hungover, I walked into a gas station on the outskirts of town to get out of the hot sun for a while. One of the attendants approached me and said, "Are you nuts, walking out there in that hot sun? Where's your car?"

I took off my shoe, shoved it in his face, and retorted, "See this shoe? It's made by Florsheim Shoe Company. I'm a professional walker who tests out shoes. I'm walking these shoes from Vegas to LA, where there's another pair waiting for me. I'll then fly to Anchorage, Alaska, and walk another pair to Fairbanks."

As hot and tired as I was, my ego forced me to walk back out into that desert sun. As I moved on down the road, I kept glancing back until I could no longer see the gas station. That's when I finally stuck out my thumb and started hitching for a ride. I just didn't want that attendant, who I had never seen before and would never see again, to notice that I was just a great big drunk egotistical liar.

As my drinking continued, my health began to deteriorate. I became a semiregular patient in the locked ward of the Veteran's Hospital in Long Beach, California. I still have some of the wallets I made during my times there in occupational therapy. I'd be a patient for three or four months, get out, and get drunk on the way back to wherever I was living at the time. But it was in the VA's locked ward that I got my first exposure to Alcoholics Anonymous.

One of the newer psychiatrists at the hospital approached me one day and asked if I would speak with two men from Alcoholics Anonymous who were bringing a meeting to the locked ward that evening. I told them I'd be glad to but didn't let on the real reason: I needed matches. The nurses had all the matches to light your cigarettes, and they put them away after supper. If I could get my hands on some matches, then me and a bunch of other drunks could gather in the men's room at night and smoke to our heart's content.

Bob, who led the AA meeting, had a year of sobriety and was a great big guy. Jack was five years sober and could fit into Bob's back pocket. The first thing I did before the meeting was to get some matches from them. They both smiled because, as I found out later, they had been in places like this, too, and knew what I was all about. As they spoke, for some reason I believed everything they were telling me. They looked like they were doing well with life after having been through the mill like me. They talked about their drinking experiences, how they got sober, and what their lives were like now. I felt some hope rise out of the pit of my stomach.

After the meeting, they asked me to call them when I got out of the hospital. They promised that AA would change my life. While I didn't follow their advice, I believe the seed of sobriety was planted in my mind that night.

When I was finally released from the locked ward, I didn't drink for a while, and I did drop into a few AA meetings. I'd sit in the back of the room and avoid anyone who tried to approach me. However, soon the compulsion to drink came roaring back and I was off and running once again. For the next three years it was more of the same, only worse. Now even the cheapest and dirtiest beer bars were slipping me a few dollars to drink somewhere else.

At the start of August 1959, I found myself living in a small, unkempt room behind a garage. The rent was five bucks a week and I was five weeks behind in my payments. I was trying to hang on to a decent job with an oil field electronics firm, but they too were paying me on Thursday, so they rarely saw me on Friday. One Monday when I showed up rather intoxicated, the chief engineer confronted me. We argued, and when I raised my fist to belt him, he turned and walked away. I was terminated that day. That night I got drunk again.

It was still dark out when I woke up early Wednesday morning in that filthy little room. I discovered I had three beers left. I drank two and threw them up. The third stayed down. I either went back to sleep or passed out, because the next thing I remember I was sitting on the edge of the bed staring out into the sunshine and feeling different in my heart and in my head. I knew I didn't want to drink anymore—not now, not ever. I stayed in that room behind the garage for three days sweating out the booze.

On Sunday afternoon, August 23, 1959, I left that room and bummed somebody on the street for a dime. I walked to the gas station on the corner and used the pay phone to call Alcoholics Anonymous. A woman named Peggy with a thick Irish brogue answered. We talked for what seemed like hours or at least until the operator threatened to cut us off if I didn't put in another dime. Peggy asked if I would like to speak with a sober man in AA. I said I would and told her where I was calling from.

In less than twenty minutes, a car pulled up next to the phone booth where I was standing. The gas station was pretty busy, with a lot of folks milling around. I was amazed at how the driver intuitively picked me out in the crowd. Maybe I looked more like a drunk than the rest.

We sat in this man's car and talked for a long time. I later learned that it was his birthday and that he left a house filled with family and friends to come out and talk with me, a sick and shaking drunk. He asked if I would like to go to a meeting with him that night in Compton, and I said yes. He told me he would pick me up at 7:30 in my room behind the garage.

That night I met the men who were to be my teachers and my mentors, the men who were to show me a life beyond my wildest imagination. They were members of the

Compton Sunday Night AA group, which became my home group, a cross section of drunks from ditch diggers to millionaires, from gamblers to neurotics. And we all fit together like fingers in a glove. We were there for each other and spent hours after the meetings sharing our hope, love, strength, and experience.

When I was only two weeks sober, one cantankerous old-timer told me I had too much time on my hands. He said I needed to get a job. I asked him where. He responded none too nicely, "How the hell should I know? I'm not an employment agency. Just go get a job."

Having worn out my welcome in the missile and oil industries, I decided to seek a position with the telephone company. I was given a series of tests by the employment interviewer, which I passed rather easily. I was outside smoking when they called me back in, congratulated me, and asked me to go upstairs for a physical. I feared I would soon be shown the door. I was still shaking and nervous as only the newly sober can be. They took my clothes and sat me on a cold examining table to await the doctor.

He arrived, papers in hand, and looked me over. His first question was, "How much do you drink?" I replied rather firmly, "I hope I never have another drink." He smiled and responded, "I hope you don't either. That's why I'm going to pass you on this exam." Thus God gave me another gift, and I began a thirty-year career with Pacific Bell.

I went to work stringing wire, but I wanted to do more. So with the company's help and blessing, I returned to school. In 1964 I became an engineer, designing switching systems. I also continued to be very active in my AA group and in service work generally. I was going on a whole lot of Twelve Step calls. Treatment centers didn't exist at that time, so we sober drunks answered the call at all hours of the day and night. It was terrific. I loved helping my fellow drunks and still do. I never missed a day's work no matter how late the Twelve Step call went. And I never missed a meeting no matter how long my workday.

One day in October 1969, the division manager of Pacific Bell called me into his office. I thought I was in some kind of trouble as a result of my alcoholic past. But upon entering, he introduced me to Dr. Rufus Walker, medical director for the company's Los Angeles north area. Dr. Walker said he had heard of me and my successful recovery from alcoholism and was looking for someone to join his medical staff who was familiar with the disease of alcoholism and how people could get sober. He knew I was a member of AA with ten years of sobriety and asked if I would be interested in joining his staff to help my fellow employees.

While I knew immediately I was being offered another great gift from my Higher Power, I told the medical director I would first have to discuss it with my sponsor and with AA's New York General Service Office. My sponsor simply asked me, "Will you be in a position to help other alcoholics?" When I said yes, he gave me the go-ahead. The General Service Office also gave me very positive feedback but did caution me about the "two hat theory." They said I would not be "an AA counselor" for my company but rather "an employee assistance counselor."

Before being officially offered the position, I was put through a series of tests and a neuropsychiatric observation. The observer was a psychiatrist named Roger. We became very close friends and remained so for the next eleven years. The time I spent with Roger was both informative and rewarding.

In the early 1970s, I returned to school and earned certification as a substance abuse counselor. However, my AA program remained first in my life, and it was what kept me grounded. My meetings at the Compton group were never dull. One night when Chuck C. was sharing from the podium, a riot broke out when gang members crashed into our meeting and tried to steal the collection we had taken up. Coffee cups, ashtrays, and chairs flew all around the room.

Chuck remained at the podium calmly watching the mayhem. After the cops left and we resumed the meeting, Chuck giggled and said, "You guys here at Compton really know how to throw a great meeting." He was right, but we moved to another location the following week. The Sunday night Compton meeting now meets in Bellflower.

After eleven years on the medical staff of Pacific Bell, carrying the message of recovery to many employees, I felt it was time for a change and accepted a management position with the company. Seven years later, I retired from this company that had given me a chance to prove my worth and help my fellow alcoholics.

During my busy drinking years, I didn't have time to marry and have kids. Besides, what sane woman would have wanted anything to do with a crazy guy like me? I got sober in August 1959, and at Christmas of the same year, I met my first wife, Sandy. She was a nonalcoholic neighbor of one of the guys in the Compton group. She was divorced and had a lovely two-year-old daughter named Terry. We dated for a year, then married, and I adopted Terry when she was four. In 1965, our son Jody was born. In 1970, a neighboring family with seven children broke up as a direct result of alcohol and drugs. One of the boys, Tony, was a close friend of our Jody and was always at our home. So we decided to keep him.

By 1975, our marriage began to deteriorate. Without going into the reasons, we decided to separate and then divorce before harsh words and even harsher feelings developed over our relationship. As a result of being kind and civil to each other, I maintain a close relationship with my children to this day. The principles of AA helped me to accomplish this.

In 1984 I met Mary Ann at a meeting during a conversation with a group of people about Gooey Ducks. I was attracted by her laughter and sense of humor. We became friends and saw each other at meetings, and at the meetings after the meetings, for about a year. Sober three years when we met, she was divorced and had three sons. We began dating in 1985 and married in 1986 in the backyard of our home by a judge who was sober in AA.

Between the two of us, we now have five children, fourteen grandchildren, and five great grandsons. We live in a beautiful home in a nice area with wonderful neighbors. All our children and grandchildren are in our lives—lives that have been truly blessed by a loving Higher Power through the program of Alcoholics Anonymous.

After my retirement, we moved to Medford, Oregon, where I continue to remain very active in AA. For example, in February 2004, while working on my Harley-Davidson with five pals from the program, we decided to start a much-needed men's stag meeting. The southern Oregon chapter of "Dog on the Roof" began the following Wednesday in my garage with these six original members. Since then we have moved twice to larger quarters, and today more than a hundred men attend this weekly meeting.

Since I mentioned my motorcycle, I should point out that we are not a motorcycle group. We are an AA group with some men riding Harleys to the meeting. And we are a very active group with many planned activities throughout the year, many involving our entire families.

How could I not be grateful for such a wonderful life? And how could I not be willing to stay active in the AA program and try to repay just a small amount of the debt I owe to so many who have come before me? Today I know that's what it's all about—to carry the message to all those who still suffer. May God give me the ability to do that for as long I remain on this earth.

"It started with altar wine and
ended with altered states."

THE STORY OF RON C.

A s I look back on my life, I believe we are all somewhat affected by our environment from the moment we are born to the moment we leave this earth.

As a child, my environment consisted of an angry alcoholic father and a mother who was emotionally crippled by the unloving, alcoholic home of her childhood. While I don't believe any of this caused me to become an alcoholic myself, I do think it led me to develop some attitudes that made me less able to cope with serious problems.

For example, I seemed to get into a fair bit of trouble as a young lad. I never planned for it to happen. It just seemed to happen, trouble like drinking the altar wine at our Catholic church. I kept going back for more while trying not to drink too much of it so that the good Father wouldn't find out. I didn't even know that the wine contained alcohol, but I do remember the feeling it gave me. I liked it, and that's why I kept going back for more.

Still, I was a fairly religious person as a child and even when my active alcoholism began. But I eventually found it very hard to drink and follow my religion. Sorry to say my drinking won out.

I was born on August 7, 1926, in Kurri Kurri, a small coal-mining town near Newcastle, New South Wales. I was one of four boys, so I learned how to mix it up and defend myself early in life. My father came from a large Irish Catholic family in Dundalk, Ireland. He was also the youngest boy and knew when he sailed for Australia at the age of sixteen that he would never see most of his family again. Back then, only the wealthy could make such trips whenever they wanted.

After marrying my mother, he became a seaman and moved to Balmain, a suburb adjoining Sydney harbor. That's where I grew up and stayed for the next thirty-three years.

I'm convinced I was an alcoholic long before I picked up my first drink. When I learned in Alcoholics Anonymous that drinking was only the symptom of my disease, I completely identified and understood. My life had been unmanageable long before I drank, and my character defects and shortcomings went right along with it. Maybe I always had an inkling of that, because the day I received the sacrament of confirmation in my Catholic church, I also took a pledge not to drink until I turned twenty-one.

I left school at fifteen after completing the Intermediate. That was in 1941. For a while I didn't do much except hang around the local park with my mates, who always brought bottles of wine with them. They would try to get me to drink, but I really wanted to keep my pledge. Still, I watched and envied all the fun they seemed to be having. They teased me and pressured me to drink constantly, so I finally did.

It was like a spiritual awakening, far beyond the buzz I had gotten from the altar wine. I felt that since I had already broken my pledge, I might as well drink all I wanted to. Soon my life was nothing but knocking around with my old schoolmates, drinking bottles of wine, getting into fights, and chasing girls. I didn't catch many girls because I became such a bad drunk.

That very first day when they handed me a bottle of wine and I gulped it down, I got drunk. It gave me a feeling of being grown up. I had also taken up smoking a few months before, and these activities combined to give me the status of an adult. This certainly boosted my ego.

While I didn't drink every single day, as I didn't always have the money or the opportunity, I drank whenever I could. With a few drinks in me, my inferiority complex became a superiority complex. I was loud and aggressive and thought I was a big man and wanted to show everybody. Maybe that's why I lied about my age and joined the army. Those closest to me thought it might help me to "become a man." It didn't. The booze stopped me from maturing.

For instance, one payday at our training base in Tenderfield, New South Wales, the Army made a mistake and overpaid me. It was only fourteen pounds (twenty-one dollars), but it was the most money I had ever had and quite a bit back then. By now I was getting homesick, so I decided to leave camp without permission and go to Sydney to spend the money partying with my mates. That's when my immaturity really showed and things really went haywire.

I kept telling myself I would go back to the base the next day, but my drinking had progressed so much that it was two months before I finally gave myself up. The army recommended me for a court-martial because I had been AWOL and was classified as a deserter.

When I learned this, I got scared, managed to escape, and fled back to Sydney. By the time the military police found me, the army's investigation had discovered my true age and discharged me.

A civilian once again, I did nothing but continue to get myself into a lot more trouble drinking. By the time I was eighteen and still bouncing from one meaningless job to another, I began to think about my short stint in the army. Generally speaking, I thought it was pretty interesting so I decided to give it another go. I enlisted again, only to experience another ride on the same old merry-go-round.

I had full intentions of being a good soldier, but my disease wouldn't allow it. I spent my twentieth birthday in jail for an assault while drunk. Since I couldn't get anything to drink behind bars, I was a model prisoner. But the army had had enough of me and immediately discharged me upon my release.

While in jail I made plans that I swore I would put into action upon my return home. I would get a job, look after my mother, be a saint, and do the right thing forever. I went down to the pub to tell my mates what I was planning to do and you can guess what happened instead.

Strangely enough, while I was still in the army in 1945, I read a story about Alcoholics Anonymous in the *Reader's Digest*. I didn't know that the first roots of AA had already been planted in Australia. Although I didn't believe I was an alcoholic at that time, I had a real nice feeling reading about "ex-drunks" helping other drunks get well and leading useful lives. But I didn't even consider looking into it.

When World War II ended, I became a seaman like my father. That's when my troubles with drinking got even worse. While I traveled around the world, I was a blackout drinker and don't remember much about the countries we visited. In the eleven years that I drank, I accomplished very little in my life. It was all about drinking, fighting, getting arrested, doing time in prison—then getting out, getting drunk, fighting, getting arrested, and winding up back in prison. Finally, one day in the early 1950s when I ran out of money, I had to ask my mother for five pounds to bail me out. The shame, fear, and self-disgust started me thinking that I had to do something, that somehow I had to find a way to cut down on my drinking or stop altogether.

We learn in Alcoholics Anonymous that God works in very strange ways. He sure did in my case, because shortly after that, I heard about AA again in a pub while drinking. I was unemployed at the time, having lost my brief to go to sea because of my misbehavior. My mates were discussing the program in a rather distorted sort of way. They weren't knocking it, but had some funny ideas about it.

Even though I was quite drunk, I remember leaving that pub thinking about the story I'd read in the *Reader's Digest* some years before. For some reason AA stayed on my mind.

At that time I was back living with my parents. One day my mother approached me and also mentioned AA. I was sort of shocked because it was still on my mind. My mother was an ardent follower of a former minister named Frank Sturge Harty, who had a radio show called *Let's Talk It Over*. He had become a great friend of AA in its early days and would talk about it on his program. He would invite listeners to write him about their drinking problems or problems with drinking in the family. Then he would offer AA's solution. So my mother wrote to Reverend Harty and received some information, which she passed on to me.

I was impressed and listened to one of his radio shows myself. I knew I had to cut down on my drinking, but never in my wildest dreams did I think that at age twenty-seven I was a real alcoholic. Talk about denial. My mother did think so, however, and kept bringing it up until I finally agreed to attend an AA meeting.

But I procrastinated. One night I came home pretty much in my cups and my mother was waiting up for me. "Did you go to AA today?" she asked. I said I had rung them up but there was nobody at home. I knew she didn't believe me, and I also knew she wouldn't let up. She had seen enough with my father, her family, and now me. So she asked me the same question every night until I ran out of lies. I finally rang them up and was told there would be a meeting that night in North Sydney. My wife-to-be, who also drank alcoholically, went with me.

The AA members there that night were mostly in their forties, fifties, and sixties. As I said, I was twenty-seven, but as I stared at the Twelve Steps of the program hanging on the wall, it never entered my head this time that I was too young to be an alcoholic. Several men told their stories. While I did not identify with them as far as their drinking was concerned, I did identify with the First Step that kept staring back at me from the wall. I suddenly had a great revelation. For the first time in my life, I knew that I was a real alcoholic. I felt the compulsion to drink leave me. That was August 17, 1953, and I wish I could say I never drank again. I didn't realize I was dealing with such an insidious disease.

Straight away I got a job on shore. I don't remember AA members stressing the need to make lots of meetings or get a sponsor right off, so I practiced halfway measures. I went to meetings now and then but never bothered trying to work the Steps. My girlfriend was pregnant, so we got married and had a beautiful baby girl. We had five more children after that, but untreated alcoholism eventually killed our marriage.

After about nine months I decided to go back to sea. Now I made even fewer meetings and lost all defense against the first drink. I don't ever recall being told to avoid people, places, and things that could lead me back to a drink, and here I was surrounded by my old shipmates and circumstances. It was inevitable that I would pick up a drink and get back on that same old merry-go-round. And I did.

I remember coming off a three-week bender and thinking about how much I had let AA down. Strangely enough, I didn't think I had left AA, only that I was drinking again. I tried to stop every day but couldn't. Fortunately, I had never lost my faith in God, so I began begging him to help me. That's when my miracle happened.

My shipmates had gone off to a pub, and I promised to meet them after I finished writing some letters home. When I posted them and headed for the pub, I had every intention to drink. When I walked in, however, one of my shipmates jokingly said he wasn't buying me a drink. I told him I didn't want one. Thinking I was sore, he said he was only kidding. I smiled and said I knew that, but I really didn't want a drink. I turned around and walked out, knowing that God was doing something for me that I couldn't do for myself.

That very first AA meeting I made was on August 17, 1953. I began relapsing in November of 1954. I had my last drink on December 2, 1954. When I came back to AA, I was still very self-willed and continued to make it hard on myself. Since I was going to sea, making meetings remained difficult. Also, I did little or nothing about working the Twelve Steps of recovery in my life. As a result, I remained very self-righteous, arrogant, filled with self-pity, critical, and judgmental. All of these character defects and others continued to manifest themselves, and I was blind to them. I walked around in the program as a "dry drunk," as we AAs affectionately call it. I was abstaining from alcohol but not getting well. This went on for some years before God intervened in my life once more.

I finally got a sea-going job that allowed me to come into Sydney almost daily. I was able to make many more meetings and hear what happens to members who do not go to meetings or not enough meetings. I began to learn much more about the program and soon realized there was more to this way of life than just not drinking. I could see that I had found a way to live without alcohol but had never really learned how to live. I was continuing to suffer from untreated alcoholism and was affecting everybody around me.

The big break in my sober life came when someone at a meeting one night suggested I try to trust God. Like I said, I had always believed in God but now realized that I had never really trusted him. I think I was afraid that if I turned my will and my life over to his care, he would call down all these calamities on me that I felt I truly deserved.

I always had the illusion of being self-sufficient. I didn't need anyone or anything; I could do it all and get it all myself. Now I was really hurting. I needed help like never before, so I started to trust God just a little . . . then a little more. I saw that when I got out of the way, things started to happen in the manner God wanted. My life was changing in the most surprising and wonderful ways.

As my faith and trust in my Higher Power grew, I also came to learn that negative things would still happen in life. That's also when I discovered that the acceptance of God's will is the key to my serenity.

My parents, with whom I now had a good relationship, died within seven weeks of each other. I wished I would have had more time to make amends. By now I had remarried, and my second wife and I had two children. Suddenly she died during open heart surgery. Our daughter, who was sick with tumors in her lungs, died at the age of thirteen. Instead of getting angry at my Higher Power, I was reminded that he had given me the wonderful gift of thirteen years of joy and happiness with the loveliest little girl you ever saw—and I should be grateful for that.

When I finally began working the AA program, I found the first three Steps helped me establish a growing relationship with God. I came to understand that he had always loved me and cared for me. The Fourth and Fifth Steps enabled me to look at myself honestly and see and admit what was causing me to remain sick—that it was not the alcohol but the alcoholism.

The house-cleaning Steps helped me to progress spiritually toward the kind of person my Higher Power wants me to be. Making amends set me free from the bondage of self and allowed me to look people in the eye and tell them sincerely of my regrets for what I had done and my willingness to mend our relationships. Step Eleven helps me to strengthen my trust in God and improve my conscious contact with him, while Step Twelve enables me to pay back to him and others for all the blessings I've received in sobriety.

One of the ways I've tried to repay my debt is through service to Alcoholics Anonymous—first in my group and then to AA as a whole. I became a GSR for my group and got elected to the area committee. The following year I became deputy chairman of the area assembly. Later I moved to Central Service as deputy chairman and chairman a year later. All this and still I knew little about the workings of AA in our community and around the world.

However, when I was invited onto our General Service Committee, I started to study the Twelve Traditions, Twelve Concepts, and the service manual and structure in depth. I was on that committee for five years and learned a lot about our wonderful fellowship and how it reaches out all around the world to help every drunk who is seeking help.

Often at our meetings, we hear members talk about those "yets" that are still out there if a person continues to drink. I believe the same thing applies if we continue to go to meetings and live the Twelve Steps in our lives each day. I've had a lot of wonderful "good yets" happen in my sobriety, and hopefully there will be more to come.

I've also seen "bad yets" turn into "good yets" if we apply the program. I am the father of eight children, and one of the "bad yets" that came into my life was having several of my kids become alcoholics themselves. It's very painful to go through, as many know. One of the "good yets" of this experience was my joining Al-Anon to cope with their disease while maintaining my own sobriety in AA. Today, thank God, they are in the fellowship and doing well.

I had a particularly bad problem with my son Patrick. He was only thirteen when his mother, my second wife, died unexpectedly. He was devastated. He lost interest in everything, got involved with bad influences, and by the time he was sixteen, was seriously addicted to both alcohol and drugs. Using what I learned in Al-Anon, I finally had to ask Patrick as lovingly as I could to find somewhere else to live. I told him I loved him and wasn't blaming him for becoming an alcoholic and drug addict, that he was a beautiful person whom I cared for deeply whether he was using or not. It pained me to watch him get worse and worse as his progressive disease kept dragging him down.

My son finally agreed to go into a long-term rehab. When he came out ten months later, he rang me up and told me through his tears that he had used the night before and again that morning. God, what a terrible disease this is. Only because I was sober and now working the Al-Anon program, too, was I able to do the right thing. I told him to come home so we could talk.

Had I not been in Al-Anon, I probably would have told him he was mad out of his mind, that he was trying to kill himself, and if that was the way he wanted to live, he should get out of my house and live in the streets. Doing so would have convinced him that nobody loved him, including his dad, and would have given him another great big excuse to drink and drug.

But I didn't say that to Patrick. Instead, I put my arms around him and told him again that my love for him didn't depend upon whether he was using or not and that he was still a good human being. We both cried and hugged each other. Shortly after that Patrick let God take over his life, and "good yets" began to happen. He got married and now has three lovely children of his own. He has a great work record, and he and his wife are paying off their own home. He is a very doting father and I could not have hoped for more. I pray each day that God keeps his loving arms around my son.

Let me share one more of the great "good yets" I've had in my life. That was meeting and developing a warm relationship with Lois Wilson, the widow of AA's cofounder Bill Wilson and the cofounder herself of Al-Anon. It was a special joy because, as I said, I joined Al-Anon myself to help my children and then stayed because I saw how it was helping me with all my relationships.

I met Lois in 1977 when I went to Chicago to visit an AA member with whom I had been corresponding. From there I went on to New York City to visit AA's General Service Office. I had the pleasure of meeting Nell Wing there. She had been Bill's secretary for seventeen years before he passed away in 1971. I told Nell I would like to meet Lois, so she rang her up right there and then. I was stunned when Lois told me to catch a train for Bedford Hills, New York, where she lived, and she would pick me up at the train station.

I shook my head in disbelief when I arrived at the station and saw a huge American car with this little eighty-six-year-old lady standing next to it. I thought to myself, I sure hope she's not driving because she could hardly see over the dashboard. But she was, and we made it to her home, which she called Stepping Stones, quite safely. I do remember, however, as we whizzed around corners, her telling me how she got a speeding ticket when she was eighty and they wanted to take her license away. She fought it and won.

We spent a wonderful day together walking through that lovely country house and across the green lawns dotted with flower beds. She also showed me Bill's studio, which he called Wits End, where he did much of his writing. She told me she was busy writing her own memoirs at the time, which she planned to call "Lois Remembers." She promised to send me a copy when it was published. She did, and it is something I will always treasure.

I told Lois that finding Alcoholics Anonymous and stopping drinking was truly a gift from God, but that I still had to work hard to maintain my sobriety and improve the spiritual part of my life. She told me that Bill, who had that marvelous spiritual experience, had to do the same thing. He always said that we must never take our sobriety for granted.

I visited with Lois many times after that, when I arrived on ships or was traveling around the United States. I would frequently stay over at the Stepping Stones house, especially when Nell Wing would come to spend a few days. Nell was like the daughter Lois never had. I was blessed to be a good friend of Lois for eleven years before she passed away. Nell and I had a friendship that lasted for more than thirty years. I miss both of these wonderful ladies, and I'm grateful for all they shared with me about AA and Al-Anon.

What I tell newcomers in AA today is simply this: Be fearless and thorough from the very start; don't do it the way I did it; get into the Steps as soon as possible; continue to study the Big Book, the Twelve Steps, and the Twelve Traditions; go to Step meetings; and by all means, get a sponsor who does all this well.

In conclusion let me say that I went through a lot of needless turmoil, pain, and suffering doing it my way back then. If my story helps one person do it the right way—trusting God and working the Steps—then all my pain and suffering was worth it.

"Meet me at my home group."

THE STORY OF STEVE P.

When I was just four years old my family moved from Michigan to Cleveland, Ohio. It has been my home for the past eighty-three years. Our family was of Hungarian descent, and drinking was no stranger to us. My dad died in a horrific automobile accident when I was very young. My drunken older brother was driving the car at the time. That tragedy made me fear alcohol to the point that I wouldn't touch the stuff until I was seventeen.

Once I started drinking, however, my alcoholism progressed rapidly; I had problems with it immediately. My older brother was a serious alcoholic, and there was never a shortage of alcohol or trouble for me. I drank heavily, as often as I could. Because I was young, I managed to remain in pretty good health, but once I took that first drink I was unable to stop.

My drinking became so out of control that in October 1943 I found myself at AA meetings. It came about after I had fired a guy who was nicknamed Red. He was a bad drunk like me. One day while drunk on the job, he had almost killed himself. I had no choice but to fire him.

Red came in a couple of weeks later to pick up his final paycheck. I said, "Come on, Red, let's go have a drink."

His reply floored me. He said, "No, I'm not drinking today. I've been sober for two weeks." I was very curious about how he had managed that. My drinking was out of hand, and I couldn't quit no matter what I tried.

Red told me a little bit about AA and invited me to go to the Sunday afternoon meeting at the Doan Group on Euclid Avenue. The plan was to meet outside, but I arrived early. I remember climbing about twenty steps to the room above the drugstore where the meeting was held. When I walked into the room, I was immediately greeted by Harry R. I told Harry I was there to quit drinking. With his loud, booming voice he said, "You go in there and sit down, keep your mouth shut, and your ears open." He was a classic Irishman and a powerhouse in Cleveland AA in the early days. What a great guy!

The Sunday afternoon meeting was a "training meeting" similar to a beginners' meeting today. I was taught the Steps at that meeting. Red and I went to a lot of meetings together over that first year. He was my sponsor, even though he had only a few weeks of sobriety more than me. He was close to my brother's age, about fifteen years older than me.

After the first year, Red and I did not spend much time together; we just saw each other at meetings. I was twenty-two years old at the time, which was very young for AA. Most of the guys in the program were in their forties and had come off Skid Row. Sometimes they took me down under the bridges to show me where they used to live. They even introduced me to some of their Skid Row friends. I knew I never wanted to get as bad as some of those guys had been.

Somehow I managed to stay sober for close to fifteen months without really working the program. I was basically just going to meetings and not drinking. During that time I married a wonderful girl, Irene. We've now been together for sixty-eight years.

On New Year's Eve 1945, my younger brother was scheduled to return from the war. He was due to arrive at midnight at the Broadway Harbor Depot. The plan was for me to pick him up and take him to my mother's house. All of our family and friends were gathered there to welcome him home.

While we were waiting, my mother handed me a drink. Without a single thought of AA or my sobriety, I drank it. I was off again! I spent the rest of the night drinking, and by the time my brother arrived, I was loaded. Of course, I embarrassed my wife and made an ass out of myself, just as I always did when I drank.

When I picked up that drink on New Year's Eve, I had no idea that I would barely see another sober day for the next nine months. Alcohol completely took over, and everything I had learned in AA was to no avail. My drinking was worse than it had ever been, and I feared I would never be able to stop again. That time I really understood what the guys in AA meant when they talked about being powerless. I was just twenty-five years old and felt hopeless about any chance of getting sober.

On Labor Day weekend of 1946, I had what turned out to be my last drink. By that time AA had really grown in the Cleveland area. Some of the members had bought old Victorian homes with lots of bedrooms and converted them into hospitals for alcoholics. That weekend I was admitted into one on Euclid Avenue and Thirtieth Street for a five-day stay. They had a registered nurse and a doctor on call. That is how I returned to AA.

Things were different this time. I loved my wife and didn't want to be a drunk. I really got involved in AA. The men I met there kept me busy every day. They never asked me if I wanted to go to a meeting; they would just say, "We'll pick you up tomorrow."

We went everywhere! I spend a lot of time visiting jails, taking meetings to the guys. Back then we were sometimes allowed to take men from the jails to meetings and then take them back afterward.

We also went to workhouses, courts, and hospitals. Old-timers back then believed in keeping newcomers busy. They knew people working with new guys and going to meetings would most likely stay sober. I was constantly surrounded by AA members, doing AA activities. AA kept me so busy that my wife got mad because I wasn't home. It took some time before I was able to find the right balance. Certainly in the beginning I really needed to be as involved as I could.

Back then AA did not use the word "sponsee" when working with a recruit. They were called "babies" because they needed to learn so much about how to do the program. Right away the guys had me doing Twelve Step calls. Unfortunately, we don't get as many of them these days, probably because so many people coming into the program are sent by the courts and treatment centers. Doing the Twelve Step calls really helped me to stay sober, and I wish everyone had the same opportunity. We always tried to go out in pairs, but every now and then I would go on one alone because nobody else was available.

I was taught to share my experience with the new man. Many times I talked with his wife and family, too. Once in a while I would even talk with his employer when that seemed to be called for. We got to know the new prospects really well and tried to get them involved right away. We took them to meetings every day for the first few weeks. They also went with us on Twelve Step calls. We always stressed the importance of working with others.

Once the new man was comfortable with meetings and

had some newer members he was talking with, we knew it was time to back away. Usually we did this by saying, "I'll meet you at the meeting Tuesday. You could pick up so-and-so and bring him with you." That would get the guy started, and, of course, we always recommended that he have a sponsor.

The Cleveland groups at that time still stressed the Four Absolutes taken from the Oxford Group. They are Honesty, Love, Purity, and Unselfishness. Living absolute honesty was critical for me, because I really needed it when doing my Fourth and Fifth Steps. I still teach new members the Four Absolutes. I have always considered them to be a part of AA, because that is what I was taught.

I have had so many experiences over the years that I would like to share, it's hard to know where to begin. One memorable event was attending the First International Convention held here in Cleveland in late July of 1950. There was so much excitement in Cleveland for this conference! I was able to hear Dr. Bob speak and attend a couple of meetings he attended, although I didn't meet him personally. The lines to speak to him were so long, and I thought I would have another opportunity some other time. Unfortunately he died later that same year.

The program of Alcoholics Anonymous gave me a new way to live; I've done that successfully for over sixty-three years. Because of my friends in AA and the support I found in the program, I have been able to overcome challenges that I would otherwise not have prevailed over.

My daughter was killed by a drunk driver a few years ago. The court asked me if I wanted to make any sentencing recommendations for the driver. Because of AA I was able to tell the judge that the man needed help and forgiveness. Since I took action I was able to be free of resentment. The man died in jail just a few years later.

Earlier I mentioned that my older brother was an alcoholic. I feel blessed that I was able to get him to go to AA. He grabbed on to the program and worked it faithfully. He died sober a few years ago. It was wonderful being able to see him sober and enjoy sober times with him.

My attitude has always been to "Keep it simple" and do "First things first." I believe very strongly in having a home group. Mine meets on Tuesday night, and I never miss a meeting. I go early to set up the chairs and make coffee. I've been doing it every Tuesday night since about 1951.

Now that I'm older, my health isn't always good, so I'm no longer sponsoring new men. But I always tell them, "I get to my home group two hours early every Tuesday. If you would like to talk to me, meet me at my home group."

"It hasn't always been smooth sailing."

THE STORY OF MARY B.

One night at an Alcoholics Anonymous meeting, I was asked to give a lead for one of the local groups. I had only been sober for a short time. It was customary in Cleveland, where I was living at the time, for the audience to be given the opportunity to make comments after the speaker finished with the lead.

During my talk I mentioned that my story was not very "good" because I hadn't reached the same bottom as many people coming into AA. A gentleman stood up and said, "Mary, I think you have a terrible story. Anyone who drank like you did, had blackouts, and didn't know if her children were fed or put to bed needs to be right here in AA."

This happened over fifty years ago. I'm still so grateful to the men and women who did so much to make me feel welcome in the program. They also helped me to understand that

AA is where I belong, a feeling I didn't have during most of my life before AA. Anyone who saw me would never have known how out of place I felt, because I came from a prominent family and was always nicely dressed.

I was born into a privileged family headed by my father, a judge. I was the oldest of four children and the only girl. We never really wanted for anything. There were great expectations placed on me since I was the only girl. Looking back now, I realize that many of those so-called expectations were only in my head. My parents loved and cared for me and only wanted for me to do my best. They did everything they could to keep me involved in various activities, everything from dance classes to music lessons and even summer camp.

Even before my teenage years, I had already become a loner. We lived in a very nice neighborhood in Euclid, Ohio, with a ravine and a wooded park just across from our home. I remember taking long walks by myself just to get away. At summer camp my behavior was much the same. I just preferred to be off by myself. Getting to know other kids and having a lot of playmates wasn't my thing. As far back as I can remember, I was a rebel.

When I was fourteen, my mother decided to send me to a very nice private school. Each day I was chauffeured almost twenty-five miles one way to and from school. Of course, I still didn't feel like I fit in with the other students at school.

In an effort to make a few friends, I created stories. It was easy to do because nobody knew me. I would pretend I had a boyfriend and plenty of other friends where I lived. During that time of fantasy and make-believe, I was not doing well in school. When I completed my first year at that school, the principal called my parents and explained that this was not the right place for me. She told them I didn't belong there.

Years later I realized how disappointing this must have been for my mother. For the next three years I became a nonentity at a public high school, graduating in 1940. Even though our country was facing very difficult times, I was expected to go to college. If I had needed to qualify for enrollment based on my grades, I would not have been accepted. But since my father had the financial wherewithal to send me, off I went to college.

During my freshman year, the United States entered into World War II, and many people my age were being sent to war. I was attending an all-girls college that was close to Western Reserve University, today called Case Western Reserve University, one of the top medical schools in the country.

My cousin was a student at WRU. On weekends he came to visit, bringing boys and alcohol; it was great fun. I was not aware of any alcohol problems in my family but later found out that both my grandfathers were likely alcoholics. Today, three of my four children have longtime sobriety in AA, and two of my grandchildren each have eight years.

From my very first drink, I loved it! I never wanted to sip a drink; I wanted to drink it right down and have another. That was just how I drank, always wanting more. One night while out on a date, I had already had several drinks when a Tom Collins was placed in front of me. My date said, "Don't drink it."

I was appalled by his comment, so I went ahead and drank it. Later I found out he was very familiar with alcoholism, because his mother was an alcoholic. He recognized the same behavior in me that he had seen in his mother.

After two years at college, my parents again received a phone call suggesting I find another school to attend. Perhaps a trade school or nursing school would work better for a girl like me, they said.

With the war going on, I thought about finding a job related to the war effort. But first, I had to help my father win his county judicial campaign. I worked at his campaign headquarters during the week and partied with the boys on the weekend. That was dating for me. I always told my parents

I was going out with the girls. My dad won the election, no thanks to me. After the election I found a job in a department store in downtown Cleveland, a large store with many floors. I was the elevator operator and got to wear a cute uniform. Back then, one really had to operate the elevators. When we reached each level I had to yell out what could be found on that particular floor. I traveled into the city each day by way of a streetcar. My free time was spent drinking and dating. The vibes at home were not good; my parents were not impressed with my career choice.

Eventually I found my "war job," working in a factory that had contracts with the government. Some of the work was top secret, which I found very interesting. My job was in the parts department counting stock. I just floated along in that job knowing I was helping to end the war.

After a while I had two weeks of vacation time accrued. Through a friend of my mother's, I learned about a camp on the shore of Lake Michigan. It sounded like great fun. I envisioned swimming, relaxing, and enjoying nature. I knew it was a "girls only" camp for ages sixteen to twenty-four, but I didn't let that bother me. I felt like it was exactly what I needed.

As soon as I arrived, I felt as if I was wearing a big sign that read "SINNER." Most of the girls attending the camp had been sent by their church for training in working with youth. We attended classes on the teachings of Jesus and the art of creative living. It wasn't long before I realized I wasn't going to be able to drink or smoke there.

Two significant things happened while I was at the camp. First, I turned twenty-one. Some of the girls in my tent gave me birthday gifts, which were really neat. The other event had a more lasting effect on me.

Every morning we had time to go off by ourselves for meditation. One morning I found myself sitting by the sand dunes overlooking Lake Michigan. A feeling came over me unlike anything I have ever felt. It was a spiritual experience.

I felt the presence of God and knew my life could change and get better. It was both a profound and unexpected revelation.

When I went back to the camp, I found a young counselor I trusted. I shared with her all the terrible things I had been doing and the mess I had made of my life. I told her about the parties, the hangovers, and the boys. She was wonderful and shared some scripture with me. She also gave me her phone number, let me know she cared, and said I could call her anytime.

Unfortunately, she lived in Philadelphia, while I was in Cleveland—too far apart to really stay in touch. Even though I had opened up to this new friend, I still didn't see the role alcohol was playing in my life.

With a new attitude and outlook on life, I went back home determined to make something of myself. I had heard about a school in St. Louis where I could learn to become an executive secretary. My parents thought that it was a great idea, so I boarded a train to St. Louis in September 1943.

My younger brother was at a military installation outside of St. Louis, so he and some of his friends came to see me at school. Once again, I went out for just a few drinks, but it got me started all over again. Over the next four months my drinking progressed, as did my blackouts. I got in more trouble during that four-month period than in my entire life to that point. I was thrown out of two different rooming houses and didn't know why. They told me it was because I was a bad influence.

When Christmas break was about to begin, the head of the school called me into her office and instructed me to pack up all my belongings and get out. So my thoughts and dreams of a career as an executive secretary died in the barrooms of St. Louis. I never even learned to type until I was sixty-eight. Before boarding the train home, I got very drunk and was badly hungover when we pulled into Cleveland on December 22, 1943.

My parents were very upset and concerned about me but decided not to say a word until after Christmas. On December 26, a Sunday, they sat me down for a talk. The talk was more of a lecture in which they expressed their disappointment in me. They told me they would not be sending me to any more schools, and I had to find a job so I could begin paying them room and board. I also had to agree to see a friend of theirs who was a psychologist.

That same evening, we visited the home of some family friends. They had a son, Ted, whom I had met years earlier when I was fourteen. Actually, when I attended the private high school and made up stories about having a boyfriend, I always said his name was Ted.

We were visiting that night because Ted had just returned from India. He was the radio operator on a cargo plane with a passion for photography. His parents wanted to share all of the pictures Ted had taken while flying through the Himalayan mountains. They were amazing pictures of places probably not yet seen in *National Geographic!*

I must have made quite an impression on Ted that night because I later found out he had told his brother he was going to marry me. Over the next two weeks, we went on nine dates before Ted had to leave for New York. From there he flew to Europe. We corresponded over the next couple of weeks. By the end of the third week, Ted was back in Cleveland and we were planning our wedding. Of course, I thought that was a *great* way for me to deal with my troubles. I would marry Ted, he would take care of me, and everything would be good. We were married five months later and moved to New York City.

As a new wife, I planned to control my drinking; I thought that it would be easy since Ted wasn't much of a drinker. I only got drunk twice on our honeymoon, which might have tipped Ted off that there was a problem. During those early days of my marriage, I was more of a binge drinker. There would be periods of sobriety between times of drinking, although they got progressively shorter.

Looking back, I can see that I was an alcoholic from the very beginning. The way I drank was not normal. Once I had been in AA for a short while, I was talking to a lady who said, "Mary, if you ever question the sanity part of Step Two, I want you to think about how you drank. It is not normal for someone to drink so much she needs to go to the ladies' room to vomit and then walk right back to the bar to continue drinking. If every time you ate tuna it made you sick, you wouldn't eat tuna."

Over the next five years Ted traveled quite a bit as a salesman, while I was home taking care of our three children. My drinking continued to get worse. If we were going to attend a party, I drank beforehand so I could get a good head start.

Just before we married, I saw a psychologist (as I had promised my parents I would) and explained to him how things were going to be all right now. I finally had someone to love and care for me. I didn't understand that alcoholism was a disease that couldn't be fixed by Ted's love.

I became pregnant with our fourth child and carried the baby to full term. Unfortunately, the baby died in utero and a cesarean was performed. At that time, expectant mothers were not warned against smoking and drinking during pregnancy. I will never know if my behavior contributed to the death of my child.

While I was in the hospital, all I could think about was getting home to have a drink. Once home, I immediately began drinking heavily. I was really nuts by that time. Blackouts became very common for me.

August 3, 1953, was a hot summer day in Cleveland, where we were living again. I started the day by drinking beer. When the beer was gone, I made myself several "old-fashioneds." After a while I decided it made more sense just to drink the whiskey over ice. By nighttime I was drinking straight from the bottle.

At about eleven that night, I was standing in the den ironing when I realized I didn't know if I had fed my children or put them to bed. At that moment, I knew my drinking was a problem. I didn't know anything about alcoholism, except what I remembered reading in a *Ladies' Home Journal* article, which said that alcoholism was caused by malnutrition. For some odd reason I had kept the article. I really think they had it backward, because it seems to me that alcoholism causes malnutrition. I didn't know what to do about my drinking, but I knew I had to do something.

Some months before, my husband had said, "Charlie is going to AA." Charlie was a guy who carpooled with Ted to work. Even though we had no more conversation about it, I remembered Ted saying that. I knew nothing whatsoever about AA, but I *did* know Charlie.

Ted was in Pittsburgh on business, so I called Charlie to ask him about AA. He agreed to stop by after work to talk to me. I had plenty of questions about the program, which Charlie did his best to answer. I remembering asking him, "What do you do in AA?"

His answer was the most important thing I had ever heard in my life. It was simply, *"Go to meetings."* Charlie left, but returned after dinner and took me to my first meeting of Alcoholics Anonymous. I'll always be so very grateful. The meeting was in an old building in Bedford, Ohio.

I was the only woman alcoholic at the meeting that night. Another woman regularly attended that meeting; however, she was on vacation at the time. It was an open meeting, with a few wives in attendance to support their husbands. I'm so thankful for the kindness they extended to me that night. They made me feel so welcome. Even though I did not go to my second meeting for five days, I was in contact with people I had met there. Some of the wives invited me over for coffee.

AA was only eighteen years old at that time. Cleveland was the place where it really branched out. Some of the original AA pioneers were still living when I starting going to meetings. Three of them had their stories in the Big Book. Unfortunately, I never had the chance to meet Bill W.; Dr. Bob had died a few years earlier. Still it was nice to be around a few of the guys who helped write the book. Meetings immediately became a very important part of my sobriety. I wasn't able to attend weekend conferences because of my family obligations.

The oldest of our three children was eight when I got sober. We had one more child in sobriety. I knew my place was at home with my family, and AA encouraged me to take care of my responsibilities. The main reason I came into AA was that I recognized my drinking was causing me to fail as a mother. Not long after finding AA, I could see that I was a good mother to my children and wife to Ted. But most important, I finally felt good about myself. It was the first time in my entire life that I was comfortable being Mary.

Occasionally at meetings today when I see a young mother with a baby, it brings me back to when I would sit at a table with my baby. That was an important part of my sobriety. If I hadn't been allowed to bring my baby to meetings, I don't know what I would have done. There was no such thing as child care offered at AA meetings back then. In the fifties there still weren't very many women in the program. At Rosary Hall where Sister Ignatia was helping alcoholics, there were only four beds for women. Thinking back to those days, I feel like a pioneer, but at the time I simply felt blessed.

At every meeting, I heard, "Alcoholics Anonymous is a fellowship of men and women who share their common problem and help others to recover from alcoholism." The fellowship is what I needed so badly. Years before when I met with the camp counselor, in essence I did an inventory and confession. If I had had a fellowship at that time, maybe I would have stopped drinking back then. I don't know that for sure, but I do know how much I needed the fellowship.

At one of my first meetings someone gave me a little card with the Serenity Prayer printed on it. I used to take that card out and really use that prayer. It saved me from drinking many times. Late in the afternoons, around five o'clock, was the hardest time. The kids were always active, I was trying to prepare dinner, and it was just noisy. That was when I wanted to drink.

Instead, I would take out the card, hold it in my hand, and let those words take over my thoughts. "God, grant me the serenity to accept the things I cannot change, the courage to change the things I can, and the wisdom to know the difference." Even today, after all these years, when something is going on at home I say the Serenity Prayer.

On the day I was six months sober, I had been asked to give a lead at a meeting. I was so nervous about getting up in front of everyone that I wrote it down on paper ahead of time. Toward the end of my talk, I made the remark that because my family is one of longevity, I might one day have fifty years of sobriety. There were several of the original AA members in the audience that night who had come to hear my story. I was kind of a novelty, being a thirty-one-year-old woman in AA and speaking for the first time. After my talk, they opened the floor up for comments. One of those men stood up and said, "Mary, about this fifty-year business: You'll do it *one day at a time* like the rest of us." I have never forgotten that we truly do this just one day at a time.

During my first full summer of sobriety, we visited a family cottage in Ontario. I was excited to be going on vacation, but nervous about staying sober while out of town. Before we left, I contacted the central office in Cleveland. They looked in the directory and found the name of a lady who lived close to where we were going.

When we arrived, I was able to locate Audrey through the phone book and we got together. She had been sober for six years and spent much of her time as a "loner" because they didn't have a group where she lived. She was only able to attend about one meeting a month. It was so good for me to meet her and learn of her experiences. It also made me very grateful for what I had in Cleveland with all of our meetings.

My life today is truly amazing. Ted and I have been married for sixty-five years. After I had been in the program for about ten years, we bought our first sailboat. We fell in love with sailing. Over the next ten years we had five other boats while still learning to navigate.

In 1982, Ted and I spent thirty-three days sailing across the Atlantic Ocean. We sailed in four countries in Europe during the next three months. When it was time for us to return to the United States, we left the boat in Europe. The following summer we picked up where we had left off. All in all, we have sailed in twenty-six countries.

Eight years ago we moved to Shell Point, Florida, where we currently reside. We just love it here! The Fort Myers AA meetings are wonderful; we have really been welcomed. I totally enjoy my home group, the Monday morning Sanibel Women's group. During my fifty-six years of sobriety, I have also been privileged to attend meetings in many states and countries around the world. Whenever we travel, we make it a point to go to a meeting.

One day when we were moored in Nova Scotia, Ted and I were headed for the laundry when we noticed a police officer. The police usually know where the AA meetings are, so we decided to ask him. He was very nice, but unable to help us. Another man on the dock approached us and asked if we had a problem or needed something. I said, "No, we're just looking for an AA meeting."

He said, "Great, I'll take you. There's one tonight." Isn't

that the way it always seems to work out for us in AA? While we talked, I mentioned it was my seventieth birthday. He congratulated me and told us he would see us that night.

A couple of hours later, we had finished our laundry and were headed back to our boat. We saw our new friend, Charlie, on the dock and stopped to chat. He seemed very anxious for us to go back to our boat. It was beginning to get windy, so we hopped into our dinghy and headed out to the boat. About halfway there we could see a huge banner attached to the rails of the boat. It read: "Happy three score and ten to Mary." I was astonished!

That afternoon we had a delightful time with Charlie and his wife. When evening came, I attended the meeting with Charlie. Ted stayed behind and visited with Charlie's wife. She had baked a cake, so after the meeting we had cake and ice cream on their boat.

There have been so many wonderful experiences through the years. I believe that I need to live the Twelve Steps in my daily life, one day at a time. Through Alcoholics Anonymous my life is on a pretty even keel, but it hasn't always been smooth sailing.

"When God has work for me to do,
the walls come down."

THE STORY OF TOM I.

The jailer was walking by, so I inquired, "When can I get out?" His response floored me. "I hope never," he said, then turned and walked away. I knew something was terribly wrong. This was not the response I had heard every other time I was locked up for drunkenness over the past few years.

When I walked back into the cell area, one of the guys who had seen the morning paper told me there had been an accident the night before. A young couple was crossing the street when they were struck and killed by a drunk driver. As it turned out, I was the drunk driver.

I think every alcoholic who has blackouts fears that in a drunken stupor, he might do something that can't be undone. Here I was, faced with that exact scenario. It's interesting that the human mind will only take in what it can handle. My immediate reaction was disbelief. I just could not accept that this had happened.

Over my relatively short drinking career, I made many bad decisions, but I had never done anything seriously wrong until now. Sure, I had been thrown in jail overnight here or there for drunkenness. But this was the only time in my life that I didn't want to get out. I didn't call my family or friends. I didn't want anyone to know where I was. Finally, one of the police officers learned that I had family in North Carolina and contacted my mother. She and my sister came up to the jail in Flint, Michigan, to see what they could do to help me.

The accident occurred on May 3, 1956. On July 17 of the same year I was released on bond, awaiting trial for the charge of manslaughter. When I left the jail, I planned to never drink again. I didn't know anything about alcoholism. That first day I just walked the streets until late in the evening. I didn't drink. I couldn't face anyone. I was just twenty-three years old and as empty as I could be.

By noon the next day, however, I started drinking. For the next few months I attempted to drink myself into oblivion every time I was awake. On November 19, 1956, I was sentenced to five to fifteen years in the maximum security prison in Jackson, Michigan. That was also the day of my last drink of alcohol, hopefully forever.

When I was growing up, I wasn't aware of any alcohol problems in my immediate family, though I knew that some of my extended family members struggled with drinking. I later learned that my father had been well on his way to alcoholism as a young man. When he was twenty-four someone he respected a great deal had suggested he quit drinking. He did, and never returned to the bottle.

I was born in the small town of Oakway, South Carolina, on October 9, 1932. When I was six years old we moved to Belmont, North Carolina, where I grew up. The first time I was ever drunk was in my early teens. I became very ill from it, but

I loved the feeling that alcohol produced inside of me. Even with the throwing up and everything that went along with those first drunks, they produced the best feeling I had ever had in my life.

Growing up, I was usually looked up to by the other kids. I had it together on the outside, but the inside was a different story. My outer self was just a front. I felt a tremendous amount of social discomfort, inferiority, and inadequacy. These feelings were intensified by my fear, shame, and isolation. I'm sure some of those feelings were normal for any kid growing up in that area of the "Bible Belt." But I personalized all of it. The more I was lectured at or preached to, the farther away I backed.

My father deserted my family when I was four, so I never had much fathering or positive male influence growing up. My mother married three more times. Her last husband was a wonderful man and a good husband to her until his death.

Eighteen days after turning sixteen, I enlisted in the army. It was the culmination of my early drinking and my overwhelming desire to get out of my environment. I had to convince my mother to lie for me, because the army required enlistees to be seventeen and have parental consent. Looking at the options I had, I think she thought this one looked the best. By then I had already started getting into trouble and was constantly missing school.

My army career lasted thirty-eight months before I was given an undesirable discharge. The official paperwork stated "unfit for military service—alcoholism." They must have figured out pretty quickly that I wasn't army material. I had been stationed in Alaska, which was still a territory, and the Aleutian Islands. Why else would they send this southern boy way up to the coldest part of the world? I was constantly in trouble because of my drinking, which by then was happening on a daily basis. The majority of my time in the army could be summed up simply by saying, "I was drunk." My alcoholism was progressing, as were my blackouts—I found myself in so many bizarre situations during that time.

On December 28, 1951, my army career officially ended. I moved to Charlotte, North Carolina, where my first job after the service was selling soft drinks. It was a new, unknown brand, making the task of actually selling it challenging work. In my first year at the company, I became the number one salesman, and I was fired the same year.

It seems ludicrous now, but I remember that on my second day on the job I wrecked one of the company trucks. I had become a good liar and made up a convincing wild tale about what had happened to the truck. I was so persuasive, I'm surprised they didn't buy me a sympathy card.

After losing that job, I took one at a cotton mill. It also lasted about a year. During that time, the only thing that occasionally interrupted my drinking was my job. I continued to get into small scrapes and was occasionally thrown in jail for the night.

During one of my drunks, I married a lady who was a complete stranger. Both she and I quickly realized what we had done and agreed to an uncontested, but expensive, divorce.

After about two years in the Charlotte area, I wandered to Flint, Michigan, with some other vagrants. I'm not really sure why we chose Flint, of all places, but I'm sure it had something to do with an imaginary "land of opportunity." It was easy to convince oneself that "somewhere else" would be the answer. Perhaps it was an attempt at a geographical cure. But, of course, I hadn't yet recognized that there was a problem.

Even though I was incapable of holding on to a job, I did manage to get hired by the Buick Motor Company. My drinking continued to get worse, and for the next couple of years I went from job to job within the automobile industry until I was ultimately blackballed by General Motors.

Finally, my life had spun so far out of control that I was unable to get any kind of legitimate job. One quasi legal job was in a bar, an alcoholic's dream come true. The dream did not last very long; I was my own best customer. Soon, I found myself picking up day jobs when I was able, doing almost anything for a few dollars. One job was pulling nails out of scrap lumber, and I managed to get fired even from that.

My address changed often. I would rent a room with whatever money I had. When the money ran out, so did I. Any relationship I had with another human was short-lived and very much one-sided. I would get what I could and move on. I had a remarkable ability to earn the trust and confidence of people; that's why individuals like me are called con men.

One day I ran a few errands with my boss from the bar. We went to the Capitol Building in Lansing, where he had to file some business papers or something. I drank quite a bit on the way to Lansing and more on the way back. I remember getting back to the bar in Flint, but to this day I have no recollection of anything after that. The next thing I recall was asking the jailer when I could get out.

When I appeared in court on November 19, 1956, it was not for a trial. I didn't want one because I had no defense. I stood before the judge knowing there was no mystery about what was going to happen to me. I was going to be locked away, and I didn't care. I have often thought the cruelest punishment would have been to be set free and told to "go live with myself."

I remember the day very clearly. I stood before a fine jurist named Steve. He talked with me for a few minutes and then sentenced me to the state prison of southern Michigan, located in Jackson. The prison was commonly referred to as Jackson or "Jacktown." The day I was admitted there were more than 6,300 inmates confined there.

Since that time I have visited many prisons across the country and around the world. In my opinion, Jackson was the third worst prison in the United States. When I was sentenced, I felt a natural, instinctive fear, but at the same time I experienced great relief that it was over; there would be no more. The way I had been living was horribly wrong; I had become a prisoner to alcoholism. I was living like a stray animal on the streets. Knowing that it was all over and done seemed welcome at that moment.

The next day I walked into Jackson Prison in chains. I didn't believe I would ever walk out of that place alive, and quite honestly I didn't care. I sat in my cell day after day in silence, only leaving when I had to. My goal was to do anything that would keep me from thinking. I had no contact with anyone, in or out of the prison, and had no interest in anything. Isolation was fine with me. As far as I was concerned, I had no right to open up or reach out to anyone.

Then the day came when I was called out of my cell by a rookie social worker. I think he had just graduated and this was the only job he could get. Of course he went by the book and asked me all the same questions I was asked by those who had talked with me in the past. He also came to the very same conclusion everyone else had come to: "You drink too much." But instead of telling me I should quit, he said, "We have an AA group here at the institution, and I think you should go."

It was the first time I had ever heard of Alcoholics Anonymous. I had never heard of anyone helping drunks. The only help I had ever received was to get patched up after a fight. A few days later, I received a paper telling me I could attend my first AA meeting on February 2, 1957. I consider this to be my sobriety date because it is when my recovery began.

When I arrived at the meeting room, an officer at the door checked to make sure my name was on the approved list. Then I walked into my first meeting of Alcoholics Anonymous. It was a "group" of three hundred men. The only thing my mind could compare this meeting to was my visits to county jails, soup kitchens, and missions. I was waiting for some guy to stand up and start singing "Amazing Grace."

The meeting got under way. There were a few readings, a moment of silence, and then everyone joined in on what was called the Serenity Prayer. I thought that was how they got the group to quiet down.

Then the speaker was introduced. His name was Chi W. He was from one of the outside AA groups in Kalamazoo, Michigan, and was a former inmate. I listened to him for an hour and knew that he and I had absolutely nothing in common. The things he shared about himself I couldn't imagine anyone standing up and sharing. It was just beyond me!

Chi ended up becoming my sponsor. Not at that first meeting, but a year later. Chi was the most enthusiastic man I had ever met. Actually, the best thing that happened as a result of the first meeting was that I went back to the next one. I think Chi's infectious spirit of enthusiasm was the magnet that drew me back.

Chi loved life, and it showed. Just the way he communicated with people had a healing power I was attracted to. I'm thankful today that he was the speaker at my first meeting. After being released from prison, he had gotten sober in Kalamazoo and became very active there. When I met him, he was the delegate to the General Service Conference for the state of Michigan. This man poured his heart into his AA work and was very effective at carrying the message and being a positive example of the program. He died on the steps of the Michigan State Mental Hospital on his way in to host a meeting. When I heard about it I smiled, because I knew in my heart that would be exactly the way he wanted to go—except he would have preferred to die after the meeting instead of before.

My experience with the Twelve Steps was very simple. It was more or less a "move at your own pace" philosophy that worked very well. Many people from the groups around Michigan used phrases like "Do it cafeteria style." When you're ready for something, take it. Don't go up in the line and take everything at once. Take what you want and go on to the next thing when you're ready for it. This is really about as precise as it was back in those days.

Today, one of my concerns with AA is that we may have gone overboard making this an "instructional process." The Twelve Steps were not intended to be instructional lessons taught by a "teaching elite." When this is allowed, we can cause more harm to our fellowship than good.

The Twelve Steps are spiritual principles we bring into our lives daily by practicing them and sharing "our experience" with others. Sharing knowledge doesn't work with the alcoholic; medicine, science, and religion have been trying it unsuccessfully for years. However, the *shared experience* of one alcoholic relating to another brings about identification and can contribute to transforming a life. That was certainly the case for me.

The group I joined in Jackson Prison was one of the more solid AA groups I have seen in my fifty-three years of active AA service. Let me explain why. We functioned as a group; we did not have an outside sponsor. However, we had friends on the outside who helped us with certain things, such as suggesting speakers to us. We would contact people who were suggested to us and invite them to speak to our group. We never had a week when no one showed up.

Some of our more serious members, over time, became what were known as "Twelfth Steppers." We handled most of the group's service functions. Like any group on the outside, we also had a lot of fun. A few of us even had nicknames; mine was "Chief Wine-head."

Our group met every week. We used the entire educational facility for our meetings and arranged all of them on our own. Each week we alternated between two meeting formats. One week we broke up into smaller groups in separate classrooms and had mostly Step discussion meetings. Each room was a different Step. We used the AA Big Book and the *Twelve Steps and Twelve Traditions* for those meetings.

The following week we would have a speaker meeting. We invited people from all over the state. This was of great benefit to our members. In many cases our members, once released, already had an outside contact and could get "plugged in" right away. One of the men in this book, Mel B., was the speaker at my fifth AA meeting, and we are close friends to this day.

Because the group was responsible for every aspect of the meetings, the members were able to get involved in genuine recovery. Everyone could participate at the same level. We believed in the spirit of rotation, and no one became "the authority." I believe that is at least part of the reason this group was successful.

When I was there, the prison population was a little more than 6,300. Our AA group had 300 members, or about 5 percent of the entire population. This is significant because a fellowship grew up around us, right there within the prison walls. It created a recovery community within the larger prison community. In addition to our regular meetings, we had small impromptu meetings with just one, two, or a few guys and perhaps some newcomers who needed a little encouragement.

The foundation for my sobriety began in this group at the prison. Much of what I have attempted to pattern my life after was the example set by my first sponsor. His positive energy and dedication to service has always been an inspiration to me. He carried "the message" by the way he lived "one day at a time." His spirit was magnetic.

Many events that took place during my early sobriety were very significant and worth sharing. One in particular marked the turning point in my life. It was when I did my Fourth Step for the first time.

Step Four reads: "Made a searching and fearless moral inventory of ourselves" (*Alcoholics Anonymous,* page 59). I had read the words many times during my first nine months of sobriety, but I hadn't taken the action.

One day a guy from the outside came and talked for the entire meeting about the Fourth Step. When he was done, I decided it was time for me to get moving. I had been thinking about it, but this meeting nudged me enough that I was willing to act. When I started writing, I had no idea what I would write or if I would be able to write. I began to write what would probably have spiraled into a long story of how cruel life was and how I wasn't really "that kind of guy."

After about two lines of writing this fanciful story, however, my life suddenly came into focus for the first time. It was a defining moment for me. I had never honestly looked at myself. I kept writing and could hardly keep up as the thoughts poured out. I wrote three complete pages of almost illegible scribble. It wasn't much to look at, but I can tell you it was the most important day's work I had ever done. Since that time I have done two more full Fourth Step inventories with Fifth Steps.

Several things happened right away as a result of that first inventory. First, I knew with absolute certainty that I was an alcoholic. There were no hidden reservations or lurking ideas to be considered. I completely understood and accepted that I was a guy who had lost the ability to control my drinking and I would never again regain it. I'll be alcoholic until the day I die. I recognized that I was a guy who couldn't drink, not somebody who wouldn't drink, but a guy who couldn't. The war was finally over! The other immediate benefit was that I became a "real" member of Alcoholics Anonymous. I began to care about those around me.

I believe the AA program is laid out in a very logical way. The first three Steps are the foundation of recovery. They are where we discover: "I'm whipped." We begin to find a Power greater than ourselves, and we find real hope.

Steps Four through Seven are about dealing with the causes and conditions. "What is it that makes me have such a weird way of relating to alcohol and the world around me? What is it that makes it so difficult for me to have relationships with people? What is it that causes my mind to turn irresistibly to the thought of a drink?" Getting to this point requires the "surgery" of Alcoholics Anonymous. It's where we face the question in Step Six, "Do I want to get well or not?"

I could write an entire essay on the Eighth and Ninth Steps! It seems practical to share something on the Ninth Step, because over the years I've seen the suffering of so many people who have not taken this action.

The Ninth Step states: "Made direct amends to such people wherever possible, except when to do so would injure them or others" (*Alcoholics Anonymous*, page 59). My personal belief is that every time I misused, abused, screwed over, or took advantage of another person in any way, I didn't win. I lost, and I paid for it with a piece of my soul. I can never be a free man, regardless of how long I'm sober, until I go back and make right those wrongs to whatever extent I possibly can.

The program of AA is powerful! Even with the amends I personally had to make for causing loss of life, this program was adequate to guide, direct, and support me in making full and direct or indirect amends to the victims of my crime and their families. Then I could find a way to live with myself with peace and purpose. The Big Book of *Alcoholics Anonymous* introduces us to the "Twelve Promises" at the end of the Ninth Step (pages 83–84). It begins with this promise: "If we are painstaking about this phase of our development, we will be amazed before we are half way through."

I often suggest to people in AA to take the time to read the Tenth Step and focus not so much on the inventory part of the Step, but on the second part, which requires action. What we find here is that the action we take to relieve ourselves always leaves us centering on others. I've come to understand through self-examination and the Big Book that alcoholism is essentially a problem of self: self-will, selfishness, and self-centeredness. Through my experience I believe it's impossible to deal with a self-centered condition by focusing on the self. A transition occurs at the end of Step Nine and shifts our focus onto others. In my opinion this is essential in order to enjoy a full and rewarding recovery.

It's not about "how I can fix myself in twelve easy lessons." It is about finding a way to deal with personal defects so that one can be spiritually prepared to engage in this business called living. It's amazing what happens to alcoholics, including me, when we take on an attitude of "What can I contribute to life?" instead of "What can I take from it?"

I experienced all of this while I was still in prison. There was no reward or blessing that I didn't receive while I was still caged like an animal at the zoo. I can assure you that creature comforts are not required for spiritual growth. I became a free man while I was locked up. I was able to live with dignity, honor, integrity, and peace while living in an environment characterized by man's inhumanity to man. Even here, I was able to become a positive leader simply because of the principles I learned by taking the actions laid out in our Twelve Steps.

I was paroled and released from prison in March 1960 with the understanding that I would return to North Carolina. They weren't going to get any argument from me. As soon as I arrived, I got busily involved in AA. That's probably an understatement. I was so busy that during the first six months, I lost twenty-five pounds! Because I had been indoctrinated into service in my original home group (the Recovery Group) at Jackson Prison, I immediately became involved doing whatever service opportunities were available for me, and there were many.

Just two weeks after my release some of the guys told me we were going to a prison for an AA meeting. I was a bit reluctant, since prison was still pretty fresh in my mind. But I was committed to AA, so I went. Two months later I was named outside sponsor of that prison AA group. To some that might not seem like such a big deal but it was a *big* deal to me. Here I was, a guy wondering if I would be able to fit in, being put in the position of a trusted servant and giving leadership to people in situations similar to what I had just left.

About that same time my parole officer came to me and said, "You're really active in AA, aren't you?" I replied, "Yes, sir." I was a little worried that he might tell me to slow down.

Instead he said, "Would it help you if you could drive?" I said, "Yes, sir, but I can't." (As if he didn't know that.) After what I had done, the thought of driving was just not something I entertained. "Well, let me look into it," he replied.

A short time later he asked me to meet him in town. Once there, he introduced me to the man at motor vehicles, who gave me a license. He asked me no questions, gave me no tests, nothing. He just handed me a license. I didn't even pay for it.

In my life I have come to know that *when God has work for me to do, the walls come down.* Not when I want to do something, but when God has work for me to do. This has been true in many ways. I wouldn't have even considered asking for my driver's license or for the service position. Five months after I was out of prison, I was elected DCM—district committee man—for my home district.

Not quite two years after I was paroled from a maximum custody penitentiary, I received a phone call from the North Carolina State Capitol. It was a man from the state prison headquarters. I had met him once when I was meeting with the prison AA group I sponsored. He told me that the state was expanding the rehabilitation program in the prison system and they were wondering if I might consider accepting a position in that expansion. My spontaneous reaction was, "Do you know who you're talking to?" He said, "Oh yes, we've checked you out." I told him I would rather do that work than anything else I could possibly imagine.

On the day of that phone call there had never been an ex-inmate hired for a professional position in a state prison system, or comparable jurisdiction, anywhere. I am intensely proud to be a citizen of a state that was willing to take such a seemingly risky step into unknown territory. That required courage and willingness to take a stand, alone if necessary.

Needless to say, I accepted the job. I continued to work in the North Carolina Department of Correction until my retirement thirty-nine years later. During my career, I held a variety of wonderful positions. Understand that not once did I ever apply for a job or ask for a pay raise, a transfer, or a promotion. I don't think these things happened because I'm "God's wonderful child." I believe that my work tells you who I am. If I do sloppy work, that is who I am. If it is the best I can do, that will speak for itself. There is nearly always a need for people who give it their best, no matter what. After many years in management, I know that there is a hunger for good people in the workplace. There is a definite shortage of good leaders and managers.

Back when I was sitting in a prison cell wondering what I might do if I ever got out, I never once thought, "When I get out of here, I'm going to come back and be the warden." It was the furthest thing from my mind.

But the day came when the head of our prison system called me in and said he wanted me to do something for him. I asked, "What?" He said, "I would like for you to take over an institution as the warden." I was shocked! Here I was, the first ex-convict ever hired in a prison system anywhere. Now, only a few years later, I was becoming a warden and a correctional administrator. For the next thirty years, I managed and developed correctional institutions and developed special programs. This was an unbelievably challenging and deeply rewarding professional career. I wouldn't have traded professions with anyone.

My life has been truly incredible. I have AA friends in every one of the United States and in many foreign countries. My wife and I have enjoyed a wonderful marriage for almost forty-two years. We have two successful children and a couple of wonderful grandkids. I have never been what you would call a religious guy, but I've become a very spiritual man. My prayers are simple. I pray daily that "I might be mindful of the great gift I have received and properly grateful for that gift. That I might just appear to be worthy of the gift and allow others to see in me that recovery is a good way to live; and finally, to make me sensitive to opportunities to be of service."

I am currently one of the busiest people I know. I am actively involved in service and in my home group, the Primary Purpose Group. Bill W. talked about there being two kinds of old-timers in AA. One group he referred to as the "bleeding deacons"; the other he called the "elder statesmen." I choose to pattern myself after the three sponsors I've had during the past fifty-three years. All of these men were "elder statesmen" and fine examples of AA.

I believe that aging doesn't mean you have to act old. When I am vigorously active in productive service work, it does not sap my energy; it creates it.

The foundation for my recovery was built long ago in my original home group. The group was solid and functioning, using the three AA legacies of recovery, unity, and service. From that group, I was able to acquire the direction and encouragement that led me to a lifetime of sobriety. Having a solid home group that follows the Traditions and offers service opportunities on a rotating basis has always been important to me. I'm a Traditions guy. In my business, my home, and my home group, I have made it a point to use and live by the principles of the Traditions.

In the summer of 1965, I sat in Maple Leaf Gardens in Toronto, Ontario, during the AA International Conference. That day Bill Wilson introduced something to the fellowship that I think is very important. He called it "The Responsibility Pledge." It simply states, "I am responsible. When anyone, anywhere, reaches out for help, I want the hand of AA always to be there. And for that: I am responsible." It is my hope that we of AA will take this pledge as a way of life. When some-body does reach out, you and I will be willing to step forward and give some help. If we do that, we will be tremendously rewarded.

One of my favorite quotes is "A miracle is when prepa-ration meets opportunity and God makes the introduction." Without a doubt, my sobriety and my quality of life today are a direct result of the service I give to others. I hope to live the rest of my life the way I sign my correspondences: "in love and service."

"So you ask me, 'Does AA work?'"

THE STORY OF TOMMY M.

During my fifty-six years as a sober member of Alcoholics Anonymous, I've been asked this question many times: "Does AA work?" I'd like to tell you my story, which I think clearly answers that question.

I was the oldest of six children. Our father was an alcoholic we rarely saw, let alone spent much time with. He was a career sailor who eventually joined the navy. He spent most of his time overseas but would occasionally be home for brief periods. It seemed that after every visit, another baby would be born.

By the age of thirteen, I was already a behavior problem. I got expelled from school for kicking a teacher in the private parts. After that, no school in the city of Montreal would take me.

In September 1939, war was declared. My father happened

to be home at that time. Being a merchant marine, he decided to enlist in the Royal Canadian Navy. Before leaving, he told me that because I was the oldest, it was my responsibility to look after my mother, brothers, and sisters.

Since I couldn't go back to school, I got a job in the local shoe factory and made fifteen cents per hour. That was good money for a kid. I only got the job with the help of my mother's friend. There was no income tax at that time, and I was paid in cash. All I needed was a government work permit.

It was understood that I would bring the money home to help out my mother since Dad was overseas. On my first payday, some guys were shooting craps. Being such a big shot, I had to join in. Of course I lost all of my money. I told my mother that a collection was taken at work to buy a wreath for somebody who had died. Soon almost every Friday somebody was "dying at work." The lies and stories became common even before I was drinking.

My next job, at a company that built aircrafts for the Canadian Air Force, paid better than the shoe factory. Every Saturday night a group of us would meet at the local pool hall and go to a dance called the Roseland Dance. I've always loved to dance. That's when I became interested in girls.

One evening I met up with a guy who was going to the liquor store. I waited outside until he returned with a few bottles. Then we went out back and I had my first drink. I don't remember what it was, but the next morning I was lying on my mother's dining room floor, violently sick. As I recall, I promised my mother that if this was what liquor was going to do to me, I wouldn't drink again. But I did.

Not long after that, I found out I could be served in the bars. I looked older than my age and was quite tall, which I'm sure was the reason I was never asked for an ID. I loved the bar environment because I was fascinated by these older men. I was learning to hold my liquor better and I enjoyed hearing their stories. This, of course, helped me to feel like a big shot and tough guy. Looking back, I believe this is when the disease of alcoholism took hold and my downward spiral began.

I can't tell you that all of my problems are due to alcoholism. I got myself in a lot of trouble even before I took my first drink. Again, I'm the oldest with three sisters and two brothers. My father was an Irish Catholic and my mother a Scotch Presbyterian. Maybe that explains my alcoholism, I don't know. There is alcoholism throughout my family. Two of my sisters and one brother have enjoyed sobriety in the rooms of Alcoholics Anonymous, as did my father for the last seventeen years of his life.

During these years, I was a rebel and got myself into a lot of trouble. I ran with gangs, stole things, caused trouble at home, and was even brought into the juvenile courts. I was fascinated with the gangsters I read about: Legs Diamond, Pretty-Boy Floyd, Dutch Schultz, and Al Capone. I wanted to be like them, wanted to be a tough guy. But I was the one who would always get caught. I used to read comic books about those people. At the end, the cops would always come in and arrest everyone. Before I got to that part I'd rip up the comic book.

In 1942, at the age of fifteen, I thought it would be a good idea to enlist in the army. I didn't want the navy because my father was in that. I went to the recruiting office and met with a sergeant there. Naturally he asked my age and I lied, telling him I was eighteen. He asked to see a copy of my birth certificate. I made up a story and told him that I was born in Ireland and the birth records had been destroyed in a fire. The truth was that I didn't even know where Ireland was. He suggested that I get my mother to sign something stating that I was eighteen. He would accept that as proof of age. So I went home and told my mother I wanted to join the army reserve and it would be only two nights a week. She thought that was a grand idea. It would help keep me out of trouble and off the streets. She signed the paperwork.

Later that day I strutted down the street in full uniform

with my chest sticking out and my head in the air, knowing that I was now important. I can remember how excited my brothers and sister were to see me and how proud they were that their big brother had joined the army. I explained to my mother that the next morning I would be reporting for active duty, but I wouldn't be leaving Canada. I suspect that she felt this might be the best thing for everyone, so she let me go.

My first assignment was in Huntington, Quebec, forty miles from Montreal. It seemed so far away. After we reported and got settled in, we were allowed to go into town. I headed down to one of the local hotels with a bunch of other army guys and felt like a real man. Of course I started drinking. After a few beers, a big brawl broke out. I ended up getting picked up off the floor, taken back to camp, and locked up by the regimental police. Before releasing me the next morning, the sergeant said, "Young fella, you had better behave yourself or you're going to get into a lot of trouble." After that, I stayed out of brawls but didn't quit drinking. There I was at fifteen years of age, able to drink and still do all that was required of me. I'd get drunk at night, and the next morning I could get up and do a thirty-mile route march with no problem. I was drinking at every opportunity, and getting drunk on most of these occasions.

After basic training, I was sent out west to Saskatchewan. There I learned to operate tanks and heavy equipment. I even got to try some Saskatchewan beer. Guess what? I got drunk on that, too.

I had completed my advanced training and was waiting for my overseas assignment. In the meantime, my job was to drive the base colonel around to his various duties. On Friday afternoons, I was supposed to drive him to his home in Saskatoon so he could spend the weekend with his family. The staff car was then returned until Monday when I picked him up. This was all going along just fine until one Friday, a payday. I dropped the colonel at his home in Saskatoon, but didn't go right back to return the car. I decided to stop at a hotel and have a beer—just one beer. Well, one turned into four, five, six, and then, "The hell with the colonel and the army." The next thing I remembered was waking up in a house somewhere in Saskatoon and it was Tuesday. Oh boy, was I scared when I came out of that drunk! I headed back to camp, and at the guardhouse faced the colonel I should have picked up. He gave me twenty-eight days of detention and never allowed me to drive for him again.

After several more moves I ended up in England. I was sixteen years old, scared, alcoholic, and alone. Ultimately I was hospitalized for nervous fatigue. While recovering, I was able to leave the hospital and did, of course, go drink. Finally, the day came when I just didn't bother to go back. When I eventually returned, I was sentenced to two years of strict discipline. This was nothing less than a living hell. However, I continued to have a tough-guy attitude, which caused me to lose privileges and be even more alone.

Eventually, I caused enough trouble in England to be shipped back to Canada and discharged from the army. It was time to face my family after four years and eight months of being away. During that time I had never written home, not even once. Arriving at my mother's house, I started to explain how I had gotten myself into some trouble while in the army. She interrupted me and said she already knew what had happened from the newspaper. She told me that I was just a boy and we were going to forget all about it.

My father was discharged from the navy with honors at about the same time. He wasn't very proud of me, but we had a party anyway—the prodigal son and his father back from the war. Of course once I got to drinking, I got violent and fought with my dad; he responded by throwing me out of the house. There I was, alone again, this time in my home city of Montreal. By now it was 1946. My grandfather took me in and tried to care for me.

One Sunday afternoon after Mass I was sitting in the living room at my grandfather's house. My grandfather knew that I loved to dance. He must have known that I was very bored that day, so he gave me a few dollars and suggested I head over to the dance hall. There weren't many people there that May afternoon. But over in the corner, sitting off by herself, was a beautiful girl. I went up to her and asked for a dance. That was my first dance with the woman who became my lifelong partner. I was twenty years old at the time, and we were married just six months later. That was nearly sixty-three years ago.

Over the next six years we were blessed with four children. Naturally my drinking continued, and I wasn't capable of being much of a husband or father. Thank God for my wife, her sisters, and my mother. Everyone pitched in to make it possible for our family to survive and stay together.

Now, I could continue detailing my life of alcoholism and wreckage, but that wouldn't really be fair. I'm not proud of the life I lived; however, these were the places my alcoholism took me. Through the grace of God I was able to find my way to AA and to an entirely new life. At twenty-five years of age there was no doubt in my mind that I was an alcoholic. Like every other member of Alcoholics Anonymous, I had to suffer to earn my membership into AA. Before I talk about my fifty-six years of continuous sobriety and the blessed life that I have been given through the program, I want to tell you about my last drink.

It was March 17, 1953, and being of Irish descent it was natural for me to want to celebrate Saint Patrick's Day. My wife was at home, expecting our fifth child. I was at work but wanted to go celebrate. So I quit my job and they cut me a check. It wasn't always easy to get a check cashed back then, so I took it to a friend's clothing store. The store happened to be positioned between two taverns. I told the lady working there a story about needing the money right away to bring home some groceries. She cashed the check, and I was off on the drunk of all drunks. I don't remember much of that day through the blackouts.

However, I do remember deciding at some point that I needed to get home to my wife. I left the tavern, and right out front was a taxi with the motor running. I got into the back, but there was no driver, so I got out, climbed into the front seat, and drove off. The rest of the story had to be told to me because I don't remember it. Apparently I wrapped the cab around a telephone pole and woke up in the local police station. This disease of alcoholism had finally made me hit bottom.

Facing jail time, I stood in front of the judge and told him that I would quit drinking. The judge requested a meeting with my wife before sentencing. Meanwhile, I was remanded to jail and allowed only one call. I phoned my sister and asked her to arrange for my wife to meet with the judge. My sister and everyone else had already had enough of me. She said, "Tommy, we will take care of your wife and family. Now just leave us alone." And the phone clicked dead.

The judge sentenced me to two years in jail. I was alone and scared. Three weeks after I was incarcerated, my wife gave birth to our fifth child, a baby girl. Shortly after that I was interviewed by the John Howard Society, an organization that tried to help guys like me. They arranged for me to meet with a counselor. He talked to me about my drinking and suggested I go to AA. He gave me some information about the program and suggested that it might help. When I returned to my cell, I knelt down on my knees and prayed, asking God to please help me.

Now let me tell you about the miracle of Alcoholics Anonymous. In order for me to see my wife and new baby, I had to go in front of the warden and the prison board. I stood there hopeless, helpless, scared, and crying, asking for permission to have a private visit with my wife and the baby I'd never seen. Then I said that I also wanted to go to Alcoholics Anonymous. They wanted to know why. I explained how things had been going in my life and what had become of me. I told them I didn't want to be that way anymore. I wanted to be a husband and a father. I wanted to go to AA, and I begged them to help me. I was sent back to my cell and told they would see what they could do.

My wife was given permission to bring the baby for a visit. She came in and placed that beautiful little girl in my arms, giving me another reason to come into AA. That Sunday morning, I attended my very first meeting of Alcoholics Anonymous. The meeting was scheduled to start at 10:00 a.m., but the weather was bad that day and the sponsor was about half an hour late. He stood up to begin the meeting and apologized for being late, saying the buses were running behind schedule because of the weather. I was so impressed that a complete stranger would take a bus to come to help a group of guys like me and even apologize for being late. It's not like we had anywhere to go. I was so amazed, I wanted to go to the next meeting. So you ask, "Does Alcoholics Anonymous work?"

Those first few meetings were what gave me the hope and encouragement to keep coming back. I learned to not take the first drink, to attend meetings, and to get involved. Those people helped me to get my life back. I was able to become a free man and be reunited with my family. I've now been a free man for over fifty-six years. This is a wonderful way of life, and I'm one of the luckiest guys in the world.

Once I was released from prison, I began to follow the suggestions at AA. I went to lots of meetings because I had no job. People said things like "First things first" and "Keep it simple." Oh, how I tried. But I'd be thinking to myself, "You don't understand. I've got a wife and five kids and no job. What can I do?" Of course they would say things like "Go to meetings and don't drink." Although it was difficult, I listened and did as I was told.

One day I decided I'd go knock on doors and offer to do odd jobs for people, cleaning walls or anything else that I could do. I found a good neighborhood to work in and was getting jobs almost every day. I'd take the money home to my wife. That was the beginning for me, and it kept getting better.

About five years into my sobriety, I received a call that my father had been admitted to the Veterans Hospital for chronic alcoholism. My mother had left him as his drinking progressed. I hadn't laid eyes on him for many years, but through AA, I knew that I needed to make amends to this man. My wife and I discussed it and decided I would go see him. I stood in front of my father not knowing what to say. Finally I said, "Dad, I'm an alcoholic. I've been sober in Alcoholics Anonymous for five years."

He looked at me and said, "I'm very happy for you, but I don't need any of that, Tommy." So I quietly went home. I thought it all through and realized there was nothing more for me to do.

Three months later he was released from the hospital and went to stay at my sister's house. One Tuesday afternoon he called me and asked to attend one of those AA meetings with me. I was able to take my father to his first meeting of Alcoholics Anonymous. He stayed sober until his death sixteen years later, and you ask me, "Does Alcoholics Anonymous work?" We became brothers in AA, but we also became father and son. It was a very special relationship for me, and I'm so thankful. I was able to give my father his first AA birthday cake to celebrate one year of sobriety. It was the first time in the history of AA in Montreal that a son presented his father with a cake. Usually it was done in reverse.

Another miracle occurred when I was able to get my mother and father together again. My oldest son was having his first communion at church. I invited both of my parents to the communion without telling them that the other would be there. That was when my mother first learned that Dad had gotten sober. I guess she thought that it was best for them to reunite. My mother later thanked me and told me that the most wonderful sixteen years of her life were those spent with him sober.

Over the years, AA has grown and changed immensely in Montreal. When I first came into the program, there were only about twelve meetings in the city per week. Today there are around six hundred weekly.

I used to live three streets over from the founder of AA in Montreal. His name was Dave B. At that time I was working for a large airline company. On days off I would go and paint Dave's house. He was a wonderful guy. I always said that if ever there was a perfect man, it was Dave. When I was painting and Dave was out, his wife would tell me about the early days of Alcoholics Anonymous in Montreal. She was also a wonderful person. I learned a great deal from them, as well as from my sponsor.

The airline I worked for eventually gave me a position working in the employee assistance program. After training in New Jersey, I worked all over Canada. I really enjoyed this job and was able to help many other alcoholics through it. In 1986, I received the company's highest award. It was presented at a dinner held on June 10, 1986 (AA's fifty-first anniversary). This Award of Excellence included two round-trip tickets to anywhere in the world. My wife and I had a wonderful time. Distinctions like that just wouldn't have been possible without Alcoholics Anonymous.

The Twelve Steps are so very important to me; they changed my life! The Step that really got to me was the Third Step. Because of it I had a spiritual awakening. It happened all those years ago in prison when I held my daughter for the first time. That was when the obsession and the desire to drink alcohol were removed from me.

Attendance at meetings has been a priority for me since I first got sober. I remain very active at meetings and continue to sponsor men. Since I worked for an airline, I was blessed with the ability to travel and attend meetings in too many countries to mention. AA truly is a worldwide fellowship and really does speak the "language of the heart."

Service work in and out of AA has been another of my main ambitions. When I had about ten years of sobriety, I began volunteering at a treatment facility. After twenty years there, they gave me a paid part-time position, which I held until I was eighty. These things have given me the opportunity to be of greater service to my fellow man and to God.

I love to share all the wonderful things I've experienced in my fifty-six years of sobriety. Although I wish the things that happened during my drinking days hadn't happened, they are a part of my story. I'm still embarrassed and ashamed of things I did, especially the way I neglected my wife and children. Yet today I see how my experiences can benefit others. I love my children and my wife as she and I approach our sixty-third anniversary. I am very proud of my family and so grateful for this life. You ask me, "Does AA work?"

Reflecting on my years in AA, I'm reminded of the many opportunities for fellowship that I have enjoyed. We would get together after meetings. If someone was moving, we would all help out. Those were the types of things we did for each other that helped us all stay sober. When a newcomer came into the program, he or she would be surrounded by people. Sometimes one might need a place to stay or help in finding a job. We stuck together and were willing to lend a hand. The guys that went before me sure did those things for me. I remember coming home one day when I was very new in the program to find bags of groceries waiting by the door. Those people really set an example of the right way to live, and I'll be forever grateful to them.

In 1985, the fiftieth anniversary of AA was celebrated here in Montreal at the International Convention. I was asked to speak. Although I wasn't the main speaker in the arena,

I spoke in front of a huge crowd at the hotel. It was a great thrill and honor.

My other favorite convention was the 1970 international one held in Miami. It was the only time I ever saw Bill Wilson, AA's beloved cofounder. He was such an inspiration. He didn't speak very long because he was quite ill and died just a few months later, but the way I felt that day will stay with me forever.

Earlier I talked about painting Dave B.'s house here in Montreal. He and his wife were such a pleasure to be around; I didn't want any money for my work. But he gave me what has become one of my most cherished books, *Alcoholics Anonymous Comes of Age*. Dave warmly inscribed it to me, and this token of his friendship has meant so much to me through the years. It's because of men like him that I want to keep sharing and giving away what has been so freely given to me.

I just love AA, so let me ask *you*, "Does AA work"?

About the Authors

After a twenty-year career in the marketing profession, MIKE FITZPATRICK has decided to share his passion for writing by coauthoring his first book with his good friend, William G. Borchert. Over the years Mike has written sales promotional pieces and training manuals for several major corporations. He has traveled extensively throughout the United States and Canada as a guest speaker and sales leader, motivating and inspiring his audiences with both his humor and his inspirational message of hope. His message to sales organizations is "Attitude is everything!"

Several years ago Mike undertook a massive restoration project to preserve and digitize what is debatably the largest audio archive related to the Twelve Step movement ever assembled. The archive contains more than three thousand original reel-to-reel recordings. Many of these recordings are the voices of the men and women who pioneered the Twelve Step movement and were leaders in the field of alcoholism. The results of this undertaking are now being made available online at www.recoveryspeakers.org.

Because of Mike's interest and research ability he has become one of the leading historians in the field of alcoholism, specializing in the development of the Twelve Step movement. Over the past several years he has worked with authors and movie producers providing material for their work.

Mike lives in Chandler, Arizona, with his wife, Joy, and their three children. He and Joy work together to operate his business as a book broker and marketing consultant. At the same time, Mike looks forward to continuing his writing career as a published author.

Both a screenwriter and author, WILLIAM G. BORCHERT was nominated for an Emmy for writing the highly acclaimed

Warner Brothers/*Hallmark Hall of Fame* movie *My Name Is Bill W.*, which starred James Garner, James Woods, and JoBeth Williams. The film, which focused on the founding of the worldwide movement of Alcoholics Anonymous, was based on material gathered from personal interviews and in-depth research.

Mr. Borchert began his career as a journalist, working first as a reporter for one of New York City's largest daily newspapers and also for a major media wire service. Later, as a byline feature writer, he covered and wrote about some of the nation's most important news stories—from Governor George Wallace barring the doors of the University of Alabama against black students to the U.S.–Soviet Union space race to the last execution in Sing Sing penitentiary's electric chair.

After writing for a national magazine and creating syndicated shows for radio, Mr. Borchert became a partner at Artists Entertainment Complex, a new independent film and production company that went on to produce a number of box office hits. These included *Kansas City Bomber* starring Raquel Welch, *Serpico* starring Al Pacino, and *Dog Day After-noon* also starring Al Pacino.

Mr. Borchert has also written a number of books including *The Skyline Is a Promise, The Lois Wilson Story: When Love Is Not Enough, Sought Through Prayer and Meditation,* and *50 Quiet Miracles That Changed Lives.*

In addition to his other films, he also cowrote the screenplay for the Entertainment One/*Hallmark Hall of Fame* movie *When Love Is Not Enough,* which was based on his book about Lois Wilson, the cofounder of the worldwide fellowship of Al-Anon. The movie stars Winona Ryder as Lois Wilson and Barry Pepper as Bill Wilson.

A member of the Writers Guild of America and a director of the Stepping Stones Foundation, Mr. Borchert now lives in

Little River, South Carolina, with his lovely wife, Bernadette, where they are frequently visited by their nine children and twenty-three grandchildren.

HAZELDEN, a national nonprofit organization founded in 1949, helps people reclaim their lives from the disease of addiction. Built on decades of knowledge and experience, Hazelden offers a comprehensive approach to addiction that addresses the full range of patient, family, and professional needs, including treatment and continuing care for youth and adults, research, higher learning, public education and advocacy, and publishing.

A life of recovery is lived "one day at a time." Hazelden publications, both educational and inspirational, support and strengthen lifelong recovery. In 1954, Hazelden published *Twenty-Four Hours a Day*, the first daily meditation book for recovering alcoholics, and Hazelden continues to publish works to inspire and guide individuals in treatment and recovery, and their loved ones. Professionals who work to prevent and treat addiction also turn to Hazelden for evidence-based curricula, informational materials, and videos for use in schools, treatment programs, and correctional programs.

Through published works, Hazelden extends the reach of hope, encouragement, help, and support to individuals, families, and communities affected by addiction and related issues.

For questions about Hazelden publications,
please call **800-328-9000**
or visit us online at **hazelden.org/bookstore**.